TRB SPECIAL REPORT 286

# Tires and Passenger Vehicle Fuel Economy

## Informing Consumers, Improving Performance

Committee for the National Tire Efficiency Study

Transportation Research Board

Board on Energy and Environmental Systems

NATIONAL RESEARCH COUNCIL
*OF THE NATIONAL ACADEMIES*

Transportation Research Board
Washington, D.C.
2006
www.TRB.org

Transportation Research Board Special Report 286

Subscriber Category
IB energy and environment

Transportation Research Board publications are available by ordering individual publications directly from the TRB Business Office, through the Internet at www.TRB.org or national-academies.org/trb, or by annual subscription through organizational or individual affiliation with TRB. Affiliates and library subscribers are eligible for substantial discounts. For further information, contact the Transportation Research Board Business Office, 500 Fifth Street, NW, Washington, DC 20001 (telephone 202-334-3213; fax 202-334-2519; or e-mail TRBsales@nas.edu).

NOTICE: The project that is the subject of this report was approved by the Governing Board of the National Research Council, whose members are drawn from the councils of the National Academy of Sciences, the National Academy of Engineering, and the Institute of Medicine. The members of the committee responsible for the report were chosen for their special competencies and with regard for appropriate balance.

This report has been reviewed by a group other than the authors according to the procedures approved by a Report Review Committee consisting of members of the National Academy of Sciences, the National Academy of Engineering, and the Institute of Medicine.

This report was sponsored by the National Highway Traffic Safety Administration of the U.S. Department of Transportation.

**Library of Congress Cataloging-in-Publication Data**

Tires and passenger vehicle fuel economy : informing consumers, improving performance / Committee for the National Tire Efficiency Study, Transportation Research Board of the National Academies.
    p. cm.—(Special report / Transportation Research Board of the National Academies ; 286)
ISBN 0-309-09421-6
    1. Transportation, Automotive—United States. 2. Automobiles—Tires. 3. Automobiles—Fuel consumption. 4. Consumer education—United States. I. National Research Council (U.S.). Transportation Research Board. Committee for the National Tire Efficiency Study. II. Special report (National Research Council (U.S.). Transportation Research Board) ; 286.

HE5623.T57 2006
629.2′482—dc22

                                                                    2006044478

# THE NATIONAL ACADEMIES
*Advisers to the Nation on Science, Engineering, and Medicine*

The **National Academy of Sciences** is a private, nonprofit, self-perpetuating society of distinguished scholars engaged in scientific and engineering research, dedicated to the furtherance of science and technology and to their use for the general welfare. On the authority of the charter granted to it by the Congress in 1863, the Academy has a mandate that requires it to advise the federal government on scientific and technical matters. Dr. Ralph J. Cicerone is president of the National Academy of Sciences.

The **National Academy of Engineering** was established in 1964, under the charter of the National Academy of Sciences, as a parallel organization of outstanding engineers. It is autonomous in its administration and in the selection of its members, sharing with the National Academy of Sciences the responsibility for advising the federal government. The National Academy of Engineering also sponsors engineering programs aimed at meeting national needs, encourages education and research, and recognizes the superior achievements of engineers. Dr. William A. Wulf is president of the National Academy of Engineering.

The **Institute of Medicine** was established in 1970 by the National Academy of Sciences to secure the services of eminent members of appropriate professions in the examination of policy matters pertaining to the health of the public. The Institute acts under the responsibility given to the National Academy of Sciences by its congressional charter to be an adviser to the federal government and, on its own initiative, to identify issues of medical care, research, and education. Dr. Harvey V. Fineberg is president of the Institute of Medicine.

The **National Research Council** was organized by the National Academy of Sciences in 1916 to associate the broad community of science and technology with the Academy's purposes of furthering knowledge and advising the federal government. Functioning in accordance with general policies determined by the Academy, the Council has become the principal operating agency of both the National Academy of Sciences and the National Academy of Engineering in providing services to the government, the public, and the scientific and engineering communities. The Council is administered jointly by both the Academies and the Institute of Medicine. Dr. Ralph J. Cicerone and Dr. William A. Wulf are chair and vice chair, respectively, of the National Research Council.

The **Transportation Research Board** is a division of the National Research Council, which serves the National Academy of Sciences and the National Academy of Engineering. The Board's mission is to promote innovation and progress in transportation through research. In an objective and interdisciplinary setting, the Board facilitates the sharing of information on transportation practice and policy by researchers and practitioners; stimulates research and offers research management services that promote technical excellence; provides expert advice on transportation policy and programs; and disseminates research results broadly and encourages their implementation. The Board's varied activities annually engage more than 5,000 engineers, scientists, and other transportation researchers and practitioners from the public and private sectors and academia, all of whom contribute their expertise in the public interest. The program is supported by state transportation departments, federal agencies including the component administrations of the U.S. Department of Transportation, and other organizations and individuals interested in the development of transportation. **www.TRB.org**

**www.national-academies.org**

# Preface

In February 2005, in response to a congressional request[1] and with funding from the National Highway Traffic Safety Administration (NHTSA) of the U.S. Department of Transportation, the National Research Council (NRC) formed the Committee for the National Tire Efficiency Study. The committee consisted of 12 members with expertise in tire engineering and manufacturing, mechanical and materials engineering, and statistics and economics.

The committee was given the following charge:

This study will develop and perform a national tire efficiency study and literature review to:

- Consider the relationship that low rolling resistance replacement tires designed for use on passenger cars and light trucks have on fuel consumption and tire wear life;
- Address the potential for securing technically feasible and cost-effective replacement tires that do not adversely affect safety, including the impacts on performance and durability, or adversely impact tire tread life and scrap tire disposal;
- Fully consider the average American "drive cycle" in its analysis;
- Address the cost to the consumer including the additional cost of replacement tires and any potential fuel savings.

In approaching its charge, the committee made a number of decisions affecting the study scope and logic and content of the report.

---

[1] *Conference Report 108-401*, to Accompany H.R. 2673, Making Appropriations for Agriculture, Rural Development, Food and Drug Administration, and Related Agencies for the Fiscal Year Ending September 30, 2004, and for Other Purposes. November 25, 2003, p. 971.

These decisions are explained in Chapter 1. For the most part, the committee sought to answer each of the questions asked by Congress by examining the technical literature and available data on passenger tire performance characteristics.

The committee met four times between April and October 2005 and communicated extensively by e-mail and teleconference. Meetings included open sessions for gathering information from outside experts from industry, government, and academia, as well as closed deliberative sessions for discussions among committee members. In addition, selected committee members, staff, and consultants met with representatives of automobile manufacturers and experts in tire materials and technologies between committee meetings.

Before the committee's final meeting, several tire manufacturers, acting through the Rubber Manufacturers Association, made available measurements of the rolling resistance of a sample of more than 150 new replacement passenger tires as well as some original equipment (OE) tires. Although the sample was not scientifically derived, the data proved helpful to the committee as it sought to answer the various questions in the study charge. The timing of the data's availability late in the study process limited the statistical analyses that could be undertaken by the committee. Nevertheless, the committee appreciates the efforts of Michelin North America, Bridgestone Americas, and the Goodyear Tire and Rubber Company in providing these data as requested.

## ACKNOWLEDGMENTS

During the course of its deliberations, the committee benefited from presentations and information provided by the following individuals, whom the committee acknowledges and thanks: Ronald Medford, Joseph Kanianthra, and W. Riley Garrott, NHTSA; Lois Platte, U.S. Environmental Protection Agency; Luke Tonachel, National Resources Defense Council; Donald Shea, Tracey Norberg, and Michael Blumenthal, Rubber Manufacturers Association; Arnold Ward, California Energy Commission; Christopher Calwell, Ecos Consulting, Inc.; Ed Cohn, California Tire Dealers Association—South; Mitchell Delmage, California Integrated Waste Management Board; Andrew Burke, Daniel Sperling, Paul Erickson, Andrew Frank, and Christopher Yang, Institute of

Transportation Studies, University of California, Davis; Terry Laveille, California Tire Report; Donald Amos, Continental Tire North America; Anthony Brinkman, Cooper Tire and Rubber Company; Georg Böhm (retired) and Dennis Candido, Bridgestone Americas; Simeon Ford, Goodyear Tire and Rubber Company; Michael Wischhusen, Michelin North America; Paul Daniels, Pirelli Tire North America; and Alan McNeish, Degussa (retired).

The committee is grateful to Jonathan Mueller and James MacIsaac of NHTSA for serving as the agency's technical liaisons to the study. Special thanks go to Daniel Sperling, Andrew Burk, Alexis Palecek, and other staff, faculty, and students of the Institute of Transportation Studies at the University of California, Davis, which hosted the committee's second meeting. Thanks also go to Guy Edington, Director of the Kumho Tire Technical Center, which hosted a subcommittee meeting in Akron, Ohio, and to Douglas Domeck, James Popio, James McIntyre, and other staff of Smithers Scientific Service, Inc., which provided a tour of the company's Transportation Test Center in Ravenna, Ohio. In addition, the committee is grateful to Ed Noga of *Rubber and Plastics News*, which provided Internet access to its archives, and to John Smith of Standard Testing Laboratories for providing tire section cutaways and other presentation aids.

Thomas R. Menzies, Jr., managed the study and drafted the final report under the guidance of the committee and the supervision of Stephen R. Godwin, Director of Studies and Information Services. Committee member Marion G. Pottinger drafted the Appendix, and committee member Margaret A. Walls conducted the multiple regression analyses in Chapters 3 and 4. The committee was aided by consultant K. G. Duleep of Energy and Environmental Analysis, Inc. He interviewed automobile manufacturers to learn about their interest in the rolling resistance characteristics of OE tires. He also provided the committee with analyses of the influence of passenger tires on motor vehicle fuel economy.

The report was reviewed in draft form by individuals chosen for their diverse perspectives and technical expertise in accordance with procedures approved by the NRC's Report Review Committee. The purpose of this independent review is to provide candid and critical comments that will assist the institution in making its published report as sound as possible and to ensure that the report meets institutional standards for objectivity, evidence, and responsiveness to the study charge. The review comments and draft manuscript remain confidential to protect the integrity of the deliberative process.

The committee thanks the following individuals for their review of this report: Karin M. Bauer, Midwest Research Institute, Kansas City, Missouri; Nissim Calderon, the Goodyear Tire and Rubber Company (retired), Boca Raton, Florida; W. Dale Compton, Purdue University, West Lafayette, Indiana; Alan N. Gent, University of Akron, Ohio; Thomas D. Gillespie, University of Michigan Transportation Research Institute, Ann Arbor; Marc H. Ross, University of Michigan (Emeritus), Ann Arbor; Nicholas M. Trivisonno, B. F. Goodrich (retired), Broadview Heights, Ohio; and Sarah E. West, Macalester College, St. Paul, Minnesota. Although these reviewers provided many constructive comments and suggestions, they were not asked to endorse the committee's findings and conclusions, nor did they see the final report before its release. The review of this report was overseen by Maxine L. Savitz, Honeywell International, Inc. (retired), and C. Michael Walton, University of Texas at Austin. Appointed by NRC, they were responsible for making certain that an independent examination of this report was carried out in accordance with institutional procedures and that all review comments were carefully considered. Responsibility for the final content of this report rests entirely with the authoring committee and the institution.

Suzanne Schneider, Associate Executive Director of the Transportation Research Board, managed the report review process. The report was edited and prepared for publication by Norman Solomon, Senior Editor, and the final manuscript was formatted and prepared for initial release and web posting by Jennifer J. Weeks, under the supervision of Javy Awan, Director of Publications. Special thanks go to Frances Holland and Amelia Mathis for assistance with meeting arrangements and correspondence with the committee.

# Abbreviations and Glossary

**Aspect ratio.** A tire's section height divided by its section width, multiplied by 100. Aspect ratio is listed in the size designation on the passenger tire sidewall. Typical tire aspect ratios range from 35 for tires used on sports cars to 75 for tires used on utility-type vehicles.

**Bead.** A ring of steel wire that anchors the tire carcass plies to the rim.

**Belt.** An assembly of plies extending from shoulder to shoulder of a tire and providing a reinforcing foundation for the tread. In radial-ply tires, the belts are typically reinforced with fine steel wire having high tensile strength.

**Bias-ply tire.** A pneumatic tire in which the ply cords that extend to the beads are laid at alternate angles substantially less than 90 degrees to the centerline of the tread. The bias-ply tire was the predominant passenger tire in the United States before 1980 but is no longer in common use; it has been supplanted by the radial-ply tire.

**Carbon black.** A very fine, nano-size particulate carbon used as a reinforcing filler in rubber compounds to provide abrasion resistance and other favorable properties.

**Carcass or casing.** The tire structure, except tread and sidewall rubber, that bears the load when the tire is inflated.

**Coastdown.** A process in which a vehicle or test machine is allowed to slow down freely from a high to a low speed without application of external power or braking.

**Coefficient of friction.** The ratio of friction force to normal force to cause sliding expressed as a unitless value (i.e., friction force generated between tire tread rubber and the road surface divided by vertical load).

**Corporate average fuel economy (CAFE).** A federal program that sets a minimum performance requirement for passenger vehicle fuel economy. Each automobile manufacturer must achieve an average level of fuel economy for all specified vehicles manufactured in a given model year. The National Highway Traffic Safety Administration administers the CAFE program. The U.S. Environmental Protection Agency develops the vehicle fuel economy test procedures.

**EPA.** U.S. Environmental Protection Agency. EPA is responsible for developing the federal test procedures for measuring and rating the fuel economy of new passenger cars and light trucks. The federal test procedures are used for new vehicle fuel economy labeling and the corporate average fuel economy program.

**FMVSS.** Federal Motor Vehicle Safety Standards. The FMVSS include regulations governing passenger tire safety.

**High-performance tire.** A passenger tire designed for the highest speed and handling, generally having the speed symbol W, Y, or Z in the United States.

**Hysteresis.** A characteristic of a deformable material such that the energy of deformation is greater than the energy of recovery. The rubber compound in a tire exhibits hysteresis. As the tire rotates under the weight of the vehicle, it experiences repeated cycles of deformation and recovery, and it dissipates the hysteresis energy loss as heat. Hysteresis is the main cause of energy loss associated with rolling resistance and is attributed to the viscoelastic characteristics of the rubber.

**Light truck (LT) tire.** A tire constructed for heavy loads and rough terrain that is usually used on medium-duty trucks in commercial service. These tires contain the prefix LT before the metric size designation molded on the tire sidewall and are inflated to higher pressures than are normal passenger tires. LT tires are not regulated as passenger tires and are therefore not examined in this study.

**NHTSA.** National Highway Traffic Safety Administration. Among its responsibilities, NHTSA administers the Federal Motor Vehicle Safety Standards, the Uniform Tire Quality Grading system, and the corporate average fuel economy program.

**Original equipment manufacturer (OEM).** An automobile manufacturer.

**Original equipment (OE) passenger tire.** A tire that is provided as original equipment on new passenger vehicles. Such tires are often designed for particular vehicles to the specifications of the automobile manufacturer.

**Passenger tire.** A tire constructed and approved for use on passenger vehicles and that usually contains the prefix P before the metric size designation on the tire sidewall. Federal Motor Vehicle Safety Standards and Uniform Tire Quality Grading standards are established specifically for passenger tires.

**Passenger vehicle.** For the purposes of this report, a car or light truck used primarily for passenger transportation. Most of these vehicles use passenger tires. Most vans, pickup trucks, and sport utility vehicles that are categorized as light trucks by the federal government are considered passenger vehicles. Light trucks that exceed 6,000 pounds in gross vehicle weight are usually used for nonpassenger commercial service. They are usually equipped with light truck (LT) tires.

**Performance tire.** A passenger tire intended to provide superior handling and higher speed capabilities and generally having a speed symbol of H or V in the United States.

**Ply.** A sheet of rubber-coated parallel tire cords. Tire body plies are layered.

**Radial-ply construction.** A pneumatic tire construction under which the ply cords that extend to the beads are laid at approximately 90 degrees to the centerline of the tread. Two or more plies of reinforced belts are applied, encircling the tire under the tread. Radial-ply tires were introduced in Europe during the 1950s and came into common use in the United States during the 1970s.

**Reinforcing filler.** Material added to rubber compounds to provide favorable properties, including resistance to abrasion. The two most common reinforcing fillers are carbon black and silica.

**Replacement passenger tire.** A tire purchased in the aftermarket to replace an original equipment tire.

**Rim diameter.** The diameter of a wheel measured at the intersection of the bead seat and the flange. The rim diameter is listed in the size designation on the passenger tire sidewall. Common rim diameters for passenger tires range from 13 to 20 inches.

**RMA.** Rubber Manufacturers Association. RMA is the national trade association for the rubber products industry in the United States. Most domestic and foreign tire makers who produce tires in the United States are members of the association.

**Rolling resistance.** The force at the axle in the direction of travel required to make a loaded tire roll.

**Rolling resistance coefficient (RRC).** The value of the rolling resistance force divided by the wheel load. The Society of Automotive Engineers (SAE) has developed test practices to measure the RRC of tires. These tests (SAE J1269 and SAE J2452) are usually performed on new tires. When measured by using these standard test practices, most new passenger tires have reported RRCs ranging from 0.007 to 0.014.

**Run-flat tire.** A type of pneumatic tire constructed of special materials, supports, and configurations that allow it to travel for a limited distance and speed after experiencing a loss of most or all inflation pressure. While these tires usually have greater weight and resultant rolling resistance, they permit the elimination of storage space and weight associated with a spare tire and jack.

**SAE.** Society of Automotive Engineers. SAE technical committees have developed standardized test practices for measuring the rolling resistance of tires.

**SAE J1269.** A recommended practice of SAE that defines a standardized method for testing tire rolling resistance under steady-state conditions at 80 km/h (50 mph).

**SAE J2452.** A recommended practice of SAE that defines a standardized method for testing tire rolling resistance in simulation of a coastdown from 120 to 15 km/h.

**Section height.** The linear distance between an inflated unloaded tire's overall (outside) tread diameter and the intersection of the bead seat and the flange.

**Section width.** The linear distance between the outside sidewalls of an inflated unloaded tire (not including decorations such as lettering) when mounted on the measuring rim. Treads are always narrower than the section width.

**Sidewall.** The portion of the tire between the bead and the tread. The tire's name, safety codes, and size designation are molded on the sidewall.

**Silane.** An organo-silicate compound that is sometimes mixed with silica to promote dispersion and bonding.

**Silica.** A very fine, nano-size particle, silicon dioxide, used as a reinforcing filler in rubber compounding.

**Speed rating.** A letter assigned to a tire denoting the maximum speed for which the use of the tire is rated (e.g., S = 112 mph, H = 130 mph).

The speed rating is contained in the tire size designation molded on the sidewall.

**Tire pressure monitoring system (TPMS).** A warning system in motor vehicles that indicates to the operator when a tire is significantly under-inflated. Some systems use sensors in the tire to transmit pressure information to a receiver. Some do not have pressure sensors but rely on wheel speed sensors to detect and compare differences in wheel rotational speeds, which can be correlated to differences in tire pressure.

**Traction.** The ability of a loaded tire to generate vehicle control forces through frictional interaction with a road surface.

**Tread.** The peripheral portion of the tire designed to contact the road surface. The tread band consists of a pattern of protruding ribs and grooved channels on top of a base. Tread depth is measured on the basis of groove depth. Traction is provided by the tread.

**Tread compound.** The general term that refers to the chemical formula of the tread material. The compound consists of polymers, reinforcing fillers, and other additives that aid in processing and slow degradations from heat, oxygen, moisture, and ozone.

**Tread wear life.** Total miles traveled by a tire until its tread wears out, which is usually defined as a remaining groove depth of 2/32 inch for a passenger car tire that exhibits even wear.

**Uniform Tire Quality Grade (UTQG).** A passenger tire rating system that grades a tire's performance in tread wear durability, traction, and temperature resistance. UTQG ratings are required by the federal government for most types of passenger tires and are molded on the tire's sidewall. The tread wear grade is a numeric rating, with a higher number suggesting longer tread wear capability. Most tires receive grades between 100 and 800. The traction grade is assigned on the basis of results of skid tests on wet pavements. Tires are graded AA, A, B, or C, with AA indicating superior wet traction. The temperature grade is assigned to tires tested at various speeds to determine the ability of a tire to dissipate heat. Tires are graded A, B, or C, with A indicating an ability to dissipate heat at higher speeds.

**USDOT.** U.S. Department of Transportation. The National Highway Traffic Safety Administration is an agency of USDOT.

**Vehicle fuel economy.** The average number of miles a vehicle travels per gallon of motor fuel (typically gasoline or diesel fuel).

**Viscoelastic.** A viscoelastic material is characterized by possessing both viscous and elastic behavior. A purely elastic material is one in which all energy stored in the material during loading is returned when the load is removed. In contrast, a purely viscous material stores no strain energy, and all of the energy required to deform the material is simultaneously converted into heat. Some of the energy stored in a viscoelastic system is recovered on removal of the load, and the remainder is dissipated as heat. Rubber is a viscoelastic material.

**Wear resistance.** Resistance of the tread to abrasion from use on a normal road surface.

**Wet traction.** The ability of a loaded tire to generate vehicle control forces through frictional interaction with a wet road surface.

# Contents

**Executive Summary**      **1**

**1 Introduction**      **9**

Study Charge and Scope      10
Policy Context      11
Study Approach and Information Base      13
Report Organization      16

**2 Background on Passenger Tires**      **17**

Tire Terminology and Trends      17
History of Tire Development      20
Tire Industry Structure      26
Tire Safety and Consumer Information Standards      29
Summary      33

**3 The Tire's Influence on Passenger Vehicle Fuel Consumption**      **36**

Recent History of Interest in Vehicle Fuel Economy      37
Examining the Influence of Tires on Vehicle Fuel Economy      39
Factors Causing and Influencing Rolling Resistance      42
Measuring and Expressing Rolling Resistance      47
Rolling Resistance and Fuel Economy      49
Rolling Resistance Data for Passenger Tires      51
Summary      73

**4 Rolling Resistance, Traction, and Wear Performance of Passenger Tires**    **77**

Effects on Traction and Safety Performance    79
Effects on Tread Life and Scrap Tires    88
Summary    102

**5 National Consumer Savings and Costs**    **105**

Consumer Fuel Savings    107
Consumer Tire Expenditures    108
Overall Effect on Consumer Expenditures    119

**6 Findings, Conclusions, and Recommendations**    **123**

Key Findings and Estimates    124
Conclusions in Response to Study Charge    131
Recommendations to Inform Consumers    134

**APPENDIX: Explanation and Comparison of Society of Automotive Engineers Test Procedures for Rolling Resistance**    **137**
*Marion G. Pottinger*

**Study Committee Biographical Information**    **146**

# Executive Summary

Each year Americans spend about $20 billion replacing the tires on their passenger cars and light trucks. Although passenger tires last far longer today than they did 30 years ago, most are replaced every 3 to 5 years because of wear. A total of about 200 million replacement passenger tires are purchased in the United States annually. Each time they replace their tires, motorists spend several hundred dollars and must choose among tires varying in price, style, and many aspects of performance. The tires they do buy will affect not only the handling, traction, ride comfort, and appearance of their vehicles but also fuel economy.

Tires affect vehicle fuel economy mainly through rolling resistance. As a tire rolls under the vehicle's weight, its shape changes repeatedly as it experiences recurring cycles of deformation and recovery. In the process, mechanical energy otherwise available to turn the wheels is converted into heat and dissipated from the tire. More fuel must be expended to replace this lost energy. Combinations of differences in tire dimensions, design, materials, and construction features will cause tires to differ in rolling resistance as well as in many other attributes such as traction, handling, noise, wear resistance, and appearance. Once they are placed in service, tires must be properly maintained to perform as intended with respect to all attributes. The maintenance of proper inflation pressure is especially important.

The collective outcomes of the choices consumers make when they buy tires are matters of public interest. The 220 million passenger cars and light trucks in the United States consume about 130 billion gallons of motor fuel annually. Finding ways to reduce this energy consumption is a national goal for reasons ranging from ensuring economic and national security to improving local air quality and reducing greenhouse gas emissions. Maximizing the wear life of tires is also important from the public standpoint of controlling the population of scrap tires that can burden landfills and recycling programs. While the handling, traction, and other operating characteristics of tires are of particular interest to tire buyers, they are also matters of broader public interest inasmuch as they may influence the safety performance of vehicles on the nation's highways.

This study was conducted at the request of Congress with funding from the National Highway Traffic Safety Administration (NHTSA). It examines the rolling resistance characteristics of passenger tires sold for replacement and how differences in rolling resistance relate to other tire attributes. Specifically, Congress asked the National Research Council (NRC) to assess the feasibility of reducing rolling resistance in replacement tires and the effects of doing so on vehicle fuel consumption, tire wear life and scrap tire generation, and tire operating performance as it relates to motor vehicle safety. Congress asked that the assessment include estimates of the effects of reductions in rolling resistance on consumer spending on fuel and tire replacement.

To conduct the study, the Transportation Research Board, under the auspices of NRC, assembled a committee of experts in tire engineering and manufacturing, mechanical and materials engineering, and statistics and economics. The study committee reviewed the technical literature and analyzed data on passenger tire rolling resistance and other characteristics. Many aspects of tire design, construction, and manufacturing are proprietary, which limits the availability of quantitative information, particularly on the effects of specific changes in tire design and construction to reduce rolling resistance. Nevertheless, enough quantitative and technical information exists in the public domain to assess and reach some general conclusions about the feasibility of reducing rolling resistance in replacement tires and the implications for other tire attributes. Effects on consumer spending on fuel and tire replacement can also be approximated.

The study findings and conclusions are summarized below. Taken together, they persuade the committee that the influence of passenger tires on vehicle fuel consumption warrants greater attention by government, industry, and consumers. A recommendation for congressional action is offered in light of this conclusion.

## FEASIBILITY OF LOWERING ROLLING RESISTANCE IN REPLACEMENT TIRES

**Reducing the average rolling resistance of replacement tires by a magnitude of 10 percent is technically and economically feasible.** A tire's overall contribution to vehicle fuel consumption is determined by its rolling resistance averaged over its lifetime of use. A reduction in the average rolling resistance of replacement tires in the fleet can occur through various means. Consumers could purchase more tires that are now available with lower rolling resistance, tire designs could be modified, and new tire technologies that offer reduced rolling resistance could be introduced. More vigilant maintenance of tire inflation pressure will further this outcome. In the committee's view, there is much evidence to suggest that reducing the average rolling resistance of replacement tires by a magnitude of 10 percent is feasible and attainable within a decade through combinations of these means.

Rolling resistance varies widely among replacement tires already on the market, even among tires that are comparable in price, size, traction, speed rating, and wear resistance. Consumers, if sufficiently informed and interested, could bring about a reduction in average rolling resistance by adjusting their tire purchases and by taking proper care of their tires once in service, especially by maintaining recommended inflation pressure. The committee does not underestimate the challenge of changing consumer preferences and behavior. This could be a difficult undertaking, and it must begin with information concerning the tire's influence on fuel economy being made widely and readily available to tire buyers and sellers. A significant and sustained reduction in rolling resistance is difficult to imagine under any circumstances without informed and interested consumers.

**The committee observes that consumers now have little, if any, practical way of assessing how tire choices can affect vehicle economy.**

## INFLUENCE ON VEHICLE FUEL ECONOMY

**Tires and their rolling resistance characteristics can have a meaningful effect on vehicle fuel economy and consumption.** A 10 percent reduction in average rolling resistance, if achieved for the population of passenger vehicles using replacement tires, promises a 1 to 2 percent increase in the fuel economy of these vehicles. About 80 percent of passenger cars and light trucks are equipped with replacement tires. Assuming that the number of miles traveled does not change, a 1 to 2 percent increase in the fuel economy of these vehicles would save about 1 billion to 2 billion gallons of fuel per year of the 130 billion gallons consumed by the entire passenger vehicle fleet. This fuel savings is equivalent to the fuel saved by taking 2 million to 4 million cars and light trucks off the road. In this context, a 1 to 2 percent reduction in the fuel consumed by passenger vehicles using replacement tires would be a meaningful accomplishment.

## EFFECTS ON TIRE WEAR LIFE AND SCRAP TIRES

**The effects of reductions in rolling resistance on tire wear life and scrap tires are difficult to estimate because of the various ways by which rolling resistance can be reduced.** The tread is the main factor in tire wear life and the main component of the tire contributing to rolling resistance. Reductions in tread thickness, volume, and mass are among the means available to reduce rolling resistance, but they may be undesirable if they lead to shorter tire lives and larger numbers of scrap tires. Various tread-based technologies are being developed and used with the goal of reducing rolling resistance without significant effects on wear resistance. The practical effects of these technologies on tread wear and other tire performance characteristics have not been established quantitatively. However, continuing advances in tire technology hold much promise that rolling resistance can be reduced further without adverse effects on tire wear life and scrap tire populations.

## EFFECTS ON TRACTION AND SAFETY PERFORMANCE

**Although traction may be affected by modifying a tire's tread to reduce rolling resistance, the safety consequences are probably undetectable.** Changes are routinely made in tire designs, materials, and construction methods for reasons ranging from noise mitigation and ride comfort to steering response and styling. All can have implications for other tire properties and operating performance, including traction capability. Discerning the safety implications of small changes in tire traction characteristics associated with tread modifications to reduce rolling resistance may not be practical or even possible. The committee could not find safety studies or vehicle crash data that provide insight into the safety impacts associated with large changes in traction capability, much less the smaller changes that may occur from modifying the tread to reduce rolling resistance.

## EFFECTS ON CONSUMER FUEL AND TIRE EXPENDITURES

**Reducing the average rolling resistance of replacement tires promises fuel savings to consumers that exceed associated tire purchase costs, as long as tire wear life is not shortened.** A 10 percent reduction in rolling resistance can reduce consumer fuel expenditures by 1 to 2 percent for typical vehicles. This savings is equivalent to 6 to 12 gallons per year, or $12 to $24 if fuel is priced at $2 per gallon. Tire technologies available today to reduce rolling resistance would cause consumers to spend slightly more when they buy replacement tires, on the order of 1 to 2 percent or an average of $1 to $2 more in tire expenditures per year. These technologies, however, may need to be accompanied by other changes in tire materials and designs to maintain the levels of wear resistance that consumers demand. While the effect of such accompanying changes on tire production costs and prices is unclear, the overall magnitude of the fuel savings suggests that consumers would likely incur a net savings in their combined fuel and tire expenditures.

## RECOMMENDATIONS TO INFORM CONSUMERS

As a general principle, consumers benefit from the ready availability of easy-to-understand information on all major attributes of their purchases. Tires are no exception, and their influence on vehicle fuel economy is an attribute that is likely to be of interest to many tire buyers. Because tires are driven tens of thousands of miles, their influence on vehicle fuel consumption can extend over several years. Ideally, consumers would have access to information that reflects a tire's effect on fuel economy averaged over its anticipated lifetime of use, as opposed to a measurement taken during a single point in the tire's lifetime, usually when it is new. No standard measure of lifetime tire energy consumption is currently available, and the development of one deserves consideration. Until such a practical measure is developed, rolling resistance measurements of new tires can be informative to consumers, especially if they are accompanied by reliable information on other tire characteristics such as wear resistance and traction.

Advice on specific procedures for measuring and rating the influence of individual passenger tires on fuel economy and methods of conveying this information to consumers is outside the scope of this study. Nevertheless, the committee is persuaded that there is a public interest in consumers having access to such information. The public interest is comparable with that of consumers having information on tire traction and tread wear characteristics, which is now provided by industry and required by federal regulation.

It is apparent that industry cooperation is essential in gathering and conveying tire performance information that consumers can use in making tire purchases. It is in the spirit of prompting and ensuring more widespread industry cooperation in the supply of useful and trusted purchase information that the committee makes the following recommendations.

**Congress should authorize and make sufficient resources available to NHTSA to allow it to gather and report information on the influence of individual passenger tires on vehicle fuel consumption. Information that best indicates a tire's contribution to vehicle fuel consumption and that can be effectively gathered, reported, and communicated to consumers buying tires should be sought. The effort should cover a large portion of the passenger tires sold in the United States and be comprehensive with regard to popular tire sizes, models, and types, both imported and domestic.**

**NHTSA should consult with the U.S. Environmental Protection Agency on means of conveying the information and ensure that the information is made widely available in a timely manner and is easily understood by both buyers and sellers. In the gathering and communication of this information, the agency should seek the active participation of the entire tire industry.**

The effectiveness of this consumer information and the methods used for communicating it should be reviewed regularly. The information and communication methods should be revised as necessary to improve effectiveness. Congress should require periodic assessments of the initiative's utility to consumers, the level of cooperation by industry, and the resultant contribution to national goals pertaining to energy consumption.

Finally, even as motorists are advised of the energy performance of tires, they must appreciate that all tires require proper inflation and maintenance to achieve their intended levels of energy, safety, wear, and operating performance. As new technologies such as tire pressure monitoring systems, more energy-efficient tire designs, and run-flat constructions are introduced on a wider basis, they must have the effect of prompting more vigilant tire maintenance rather than fostering more complacency in this regard. Motorists must be alerted to the fact that even small losses in inflation pressure can greatly reduce tire life, fuel economy, safety, and operating performance. A strong message urging vigilant maintenance of inflation must therefore be a central part of communicating information on the energy performance of tires to motorists.

# 1

# Introduction

During 2005, gasoline and diesel prices, adjusted for inflation, rose to levels not experienced in the United States in a quarter century. For a growing number of Americans, the price of motor fuel has become a real financial concern. Whether fuel prices will stabilize or fluctuate remains to be seen, but one apparent outcome of recent price instability is renewed interest among consumers and policy makers in vehicle fuel economy. Motor vehicles account for about half of the nation's petroleum usage, and about three-quarters of this fuel goes to the 220 million cars and light-duty trucks in the nation's passenger vehicle fleet (Davis and Diegel 2004, 1-17, 1-18, 3-7, 4-2, 4-3).[1] In traveling some 2,600 billion miles, these vehicles burn about 130 billion gallons of gasoline and diesel fuel each year, or about 600 gallons per vehicle on average (Davis and Diegel 2004, 4-2, 4-3). In terms of fuel economy, passenger vehicles in the fleet average about 20 miles per gallon (mpg), which includes the 22.1 mpg averaged by cars and the 17.6 mpg averaged by light trucks (Davis and Diegel 2004, 4-2, 4-3).

Many variables affect vehicle fuel economy, among them the vehicle's weight, aerodynamics, engine, driveline, and accessory load. The vehicle's tires also influence fuel economy by causing rolling resistance, which consumes energy and thus reduces fuel economy. Anyone who has pedaled a bicycle with tires low on air can attest to the added work required to overcome the increase in rolling resistance. Even if it is prop-

---

[1] Statistics on passenger vehicle populations, travel, and motor fuel use referenced in this report are drawn from the U.S. Department of Energy's *Transportation Energy Data Book*, which is cited as Davis and Diegel 2004. The statistics in the *Data Book* are derived from several sources, including *Highway Statistics*, published annually by the Federal Highway Administration of the U.S. Department of Transportation. The data are for 2002 and 2003, which were the most recent years available for these statistics when this report was prepared.

erly inflated, a bicycle tire exhibits rolling resistance that varies with the tire's size, construction, and materials. This variability, even when slight, can be noticeable to the frequent bicyclist. However, large variations in the rolling resistance of tires used on motor vehicles may go completely unnoticed by the driver, since the vehicle's engine does all the work. Despite paying the price of more frequent refueling, the driver may never make a connection between the tires and the rate of fuel consumption.

This study examines the contribution of tires to vehicle fuel economy, the variability in energy performance among tires, and technical and economic issues associated with means of improving tire energy performance. The focus is on replacement tires designed for passenger cars as well as vehicles defined as light trucks and used mainly for personal transportation.

Congress requested the study, presumably to help inform both consumers and policy makers. Most motorists will replace their tires every 3 to 5 years, but few are likely to know the effects of their tire purchases on the rate of fuel consumption of their vehicles, because little consumer information is available on this tire characteristic. While the extent of consumer interest in tire energy performance is unclear, it is reasonable to assume that motorists care more about this characteristic when fuel prices are high or rising. With respect to the public interest overall, the approximately 200 million replacement tires that are purchased each year by U.S. consumers have many collective effects on society. Most of the 160 million to 175 million passenger vehicles in the United States that are more than 3 or 4 years old are equipped with replacement tires (Davis and Diegel 2004, 3-9, 3-10). These vehicles make up about 75 percent of the passenger vehicle fleet. Replacement tires thus affect not only motor fuel consumption in the aggregate but also vehicle safety performance and the nation's solid waste and recycling streams. Consequently, passenger tires have long been the subject of federal, state, and local regulations and environmental policies.

## STUDY CHARGE AND SCOPE

Congress requested this study of national tire efficiency. The language of the request, which constitutes the study's statement of task, can be found in the Preface. In short, Congress called for an evaluation of how lowering the rolling resistance of replacement tires used on passenger cars and light trucks could affect

- Motor fuel consumption nationally;
- Tire wear life and the generation of scrap tires;
- Tire performance characteristics, including those affecting vehicle safety; and
- Total consumer spending on tires and fuel.

The study request further urges that consideration be given to the "average American drive cycle." This cycle was not defined, but it suggests that the effects listed above should be considered with ample regard for how tires are used and maintained in practice during their lifetime of service.

The request focuses on replacement tires as opposed to original equipment (OE) tires. Replacement tires are purchased directly by consumers, and they are subject to market and regulatory influences different from those of OE tires supplied to automobile manufacturers. The study's focus on replacement tires, however, does not mean that OE tires are excluded from consideration. Indeed, much can be learned from OE tires. Federal fuel economy regulations that apply to new passenger vehicles have prompted automobile manufacturers to demand tires that will exhibit lower rolling resistance when new equipment on vehicles is subjected to fuel economy testing.[2] Moreover, because OE tires are designed specifically for the vehicles to which they are supplied, motorists may have an interest in replacing them with aftermarket tires that will offer many of the same characteristics and capabilities, including energy performance.

## POLICY CONTEXT

A decade ago, the National Highway Traffic Safety Administration (NHTSA) proposed a fuel economy rating for passenger tires—one that would provide tire buyers with a performance grade molded on the tire sidewall.[3] Although the rating system was not adopted, the ensuing debate

---

[2] Federal fuel economy standards apply only to new vehicles and do not govern the energy performance of aftermarket components or maintenance of fuel economy over the lifetime of a vehicle's operation.

[3] 59 CFR 19686, 60 CFR 27472, and 61 CFR 47437.

revealed gaps in the information available concerning tire rolling resistance levels and the effects of lowering rolling resistance on tire wear resistance, other aspects of tire operating performance, and vehicle fuel use. Federal legislative proposals have emerged periodically ever since, including an amendment to the 2005 Energy Policy Act—later withdrawn—calling on NHTSA to establish a national tire efficiency program to set policies and procedures for tire fuel economy testing and labeling and for promoting the sale of replacement tires that consume less energy.

As interest in tire energy performance has fluctuated at the federal level, some state governments and private organizations have taken steps to promote improvements. In 2003, California enacted a law (AB 844) requiring tire manufacturers to report the rolling resistance properties and fuel economy effects of replacement tires sold in the state. Charged with implementing the law, the California Energy Commission, with financial support from the California Integrated Waste Management Board, has been gathering rolling resistance information and other data on passenger tires. The purpose is to assess the feasibility and desirability of establishing a consumer information program or defining an energy performance standard for replacement tires sold in California.

Surprisingly, tire energy performance has received even less attention in Europe and Japan than in the United States. A strong interest in high-performance tires by European and Japanese motorists is one reason for this situation. Nevertheless, since 1977, Germany has administered the "Blue Angel" environmental labeling program, whereby companies voluntarily submit their products for testing and recognition as "environmentally sound." Passenger tires are one of nearly 100 product categories in the German program, and they are tested for several properties, including noise emissions, wet traction, hydroplaning, and rolling resistance.

Seeking ways to improve the energy performance of individual motor vehicle components, the International Energy Agency (IEA) convened a workshop in November 2005 to examine how rolling resistance is measured in tires and how these measurements can translate into reductions in vehicle fuel consumption. Workshop participants—drawn mostly from Europe and the United States—discussed the grounds for and feasibility of internationally uniform procedures for rating the energy performance of tires. The IEA activity may be indicative of a growing interest in tire energy performance abroad as well as in the United States.[4]

## STUDY APPROACH AND INFORMATION BASE

Much of the technical literature on tire rolling resistance dates from the mid-1970s to mid-1980s and coincides with rising energy prices and the heightened consumer and government interest in vehicle fuel economy at that time. The studies from that era describe and document the effects of changes in tire designs, dimensions, materials, and operating conditions on rolling resistance. These studies consisted mainly of laboratory experiments and simulations. Much of what is known today about the effects of individual tire components (e.g., tread band, sidewall, and bead) and operating conditions (e.g., tire pressure, vehicle speed, and load) on tire energy performance originated from this earlier period.

Data characterizing the rolling resistance of today's passenger tires— those on the market and in use on the nation's highways—are more difficult to obtain. Such data are essential, however, in confirming relationships observed in past experiments and in characterizing rolling resistance levels in the current tire population and their association with other tire performance characteristics. Tires are designed and constructed in several ways that can affect their rolling resistance as well as other characteristics such as wear resistance and traction. Tires on the market vary in rolling resistance. How these differences in rolling resistance relate to other aspects of tire operating performance and cost is an empirical question that can be addressed by examining tires that are available and in common use today.

Data on rolling resistance characteristics for large samples of passenger tires proved scarce. Measurements from only a few hundred tires have been reported publicly since the mass introduction of radial-ply tires more than three decades ago. These data, derived from varied sources such as the U.S. Environmental Protection Agency and *Consumer Reports* magazine, are reported to the extent possible, but some are not analyzed any further because of uncertainties and limitations in measurement and

---

[4] Presentations and a summary of the IEA conference can be found at www.iea.org.

sampling methods. Some of the data sets contain additional information on tire characteristics such as tread wear, traction, and price, but most do not.

The largest and most current set of data containing measurements of tire rolling resistance was made available by three tire manufacturers during the course of the study. These data are analyzed statistically in this report, although the results are accompanied by a number of caveats concerning their relevance to the full population of tires on the replacement market. The majority of the data came from one tire manufacturer; hence, the degree to which the data are representative of tires on the market is not established. The rolling resistance values reported were derived from tests performed on single tire specimens for each tire model and size. Ideally, more tires would have been tested from each tire model to enhance measurement accuracy and ensure the absence of anomalous results. Standardized rolling resistance measurement methods were used, but variations in testing machinery could have affected the comparability of the data reported by different tire companies. Although the sampling was not scientific and the method of data collection was not fully satisfactory, the committee believes that the tire company data, when properly characterized and coupled with information from other replacement tire samples and information obtained by the committee on OE tires, provide useful insights into the rolling resistance and other characteristics of new passenger tires.[5]

With this information in hand, the committee sought to address the questions asked in the study charge. However, the data provided by tire manufacturers were not made available to the committee until late in the study, which limited the statistical analyses that could be performed. The analyses that were performed are intended to uncover general patterns. Some elements of the questions asked by Congress required interpretation and clarification by the committee—for example, in determining what constitutes "technically feasible" and what is meant by the "average American drive cycle." One could maintain that only those

---

[5] The State of California is sponsoring the testing of approximately 120 passenger tires for rolling resistance. It is also testing a portion of the sampled tires for other characteristics such as wet traction and wear resistance. The test results, expected to be available in August 2006, may shed additional light on the issues examined in this study.

tires already for sale are demonstrably "feasible" from both a technical and economic standpoint. Still, technologies throughout the development process can be assessed for technical and economic feasibility. With regard to the "average American drive cycle," there are many different types of drive cycles. Distilling all U.S. driving activity into a single representative cycle would be a formidable task. Among the many complicating factors are the variability in trip durations and speeds; vehicle types and applications; ambient temperatures, rain, and snow; tire inflation pressures and loads; and road surface types, textures, and temperatures. The committee decided that the most appropriate "average American drive cycle" is simply total miles traveled divided by total fuel consumed by passenger vehicles, since energy expended on rolling resistance is more a function of miles traveled than travel speed.

The meaning of tire "performance" also required some interpretation. An examination of all aspects of tire performance would risk becoming a wide-ranging assessment of all potential relationships between rolling resistance and the multitude of tire qualities that are of interest to motorists, such as noise, handling, appearance, speed capability, and ride comfort, as well as traction and wear resistance. The committee could not think of a meaningful way to assess all possible effects. The dimensions of tire performance specifically mentioned in the congressional charge are energy (fuel), safety, and wear performance. Accordingly, the committee chose to focus the study on those three aspects of performance, with traction deemed to be the characteristic most relevant to assessing effects on safety performance.

The study did not examine all societal effects associated with improving tire energy performance. The focus is limited to direct effects on the consumer. The consumer in this case is the U.S. motorist. Congress asked for estimates of the effects of low-rolling-resistance replacement tires on consumer expenditures for tires and fuel. Society as a whole is also affected by changes in the rate of scrap tire generation and motor fuel consumption, as well as the energy and materials used in tire production. Tracing through and quantifying these broader societal effects, however, would require consideration of outcomes ranging from local air pollution to greenhouse gas buildup. While such a broader accounting of effects may be relevant to policy making, it is beyond the scope and capabilities of this study.

## REPORT ORGANIZATION

Chapter 2 provides context and background on the passenger tire's development, use, and regulation. Chapter 3 examines tire rolling resistance and its effect on motor vehicle fuel economy. It examines the sources of rolling resistance, methods for testing and measuring rolling resistance, and the range and variability in rolling resistance among new passenger tires. The effects of incremental changes in rolling resistance on motor vehicle fuel economy and consumption are also calculated. Chapter 4 examines relationships among rolling resistance, tire wear life, and traction, including the latter's bearing on motor vehicle safety. Chapter 5 examines and estimates the effects of lower rolling resistance on consumer expenditures on fuel and tires. The study's key findings, conclusions, and recommendations are presented in Chapter 6.

## REFERENCE

Davis, S. C., and S. W. Diegel. 2004. *Transportation Energy Data Book: Edition 24.* Report ORNL-6973. Center for Transportation Analysis, Oak Ridge National Laboratory, Oak Ridge, Tenn.

# 2

# Background on Passenger Tires

This chapter begins with an introduction and overview of basic terminology and trends pertaining to passenger tires and their use in the United States. The introductory discussion is followed by background on the development of tires, the structure of the tire industry, and tire regulations and standards.

## TIRE TERMINOLOGY AND TRENDS

Pneumatic, or air-filled, tires are used on vehicles as diverse in form and function as airplanes, bicycles, tractors, and race cars. Accordingly, they encompass a wide range of sizes, designs, materials, and construction types. Nevertheless, structural elements that are common to all of these tires are the casing, bead, and tread band.

The casing—often called the carcass—is the structural frame of the tire. It usually consists of directionally oriented cords banded together by rubber into layers, called plies, which give the tire strength and stiffness while retaining flexibility. The number of plies is determined by tire type, size, inflation pressure, and intended application. Plies oriented mainly from side to side are "radial," while plies oriented diagonally are "bias." In the area where the tread is applied, the plies in the radial casing are usually covered by a relatively stiff steel belt or a steel belt covered by a circumferential nylon cap ply. The steel belt is made by using fine wire twisted into cables as cords. For the inflated tire to be retained on the wheel rim, the plies are anchored around circumferential hoops made of multiple strands of fine, high-tensile wire located at the inner edges of the two sidewalls where they mate with the rim. These two hoops, called beads, are pressed against the rim flange by inflation pressure, thereby seating and sealing the tire on the rim. Encircling the tire is the tread. This is a thick band of rubber that forms the tire surface, from its crown (its largest radius) to its shoulders (the areas in which the tread transitions to the sidewalls).

The tread is the only part of the tire that comes in contact with the road surface during normal driving. The tread band consists of a grooved section on top of a base. The tread's design, including its grooved pattern, helps in the removal of road surface water and other contaminants from under the tire while maintaining an adequate level of frictional adhesion between the tire and road to generate torque, cornering, and braking forces under a wide range of operating conditions. For most passenger tires, the grooves start out 9/32 to 13/32 inch deep. Tires are normally considered worn when only 2/32 inch of tread remains.

Most steel-belted radial passenger tires weigh more than 20 pounds, and they can exceed 50 pounds. The steel typically makes up about 15 percent of the total weight, the cord material another 5 percent, and the rubber compound in the carcass and tread about 80 percent (Modern Tire Dealer 2006, 51). Most of the rubber compound's weight is from natural and synthetic polymers and reinforcing fillers. Other materials added to the compound during processing, such as oils, can contribute 3 to 25 percent of its weight. Because these compounding materials can account for about half of a tire's total production cost, fluctuations in material prices can have important effects on tire retail prices (Modern Tire Dealer 2006, 46).

The largest application of pneumatic tires is on highway vehicles, which consist of heavy and medium trucks, commercial light trucks, and cars and light trucks used as passenger vehicles. Heavy and medium trucks range from buses to tractor-trailers and construction vehicles. Their tires are designed for heavy workloads, long-distance travel, and rough terrain. Commercial light trucks include many full-size pickups and vans, as well as some SUVs. Their tires are designed mainly for rough terrain and heavy loads. Cars and light-duty trucks used for passenger transportation are the most common vehicles on the highway. Their tires are designed mainly for ride comfort, traction, handling, and wear life, as well as appearance and affordability.

The focus of this study is on tires used on passenger cars and light-duty trucks. The federal government defines and regulates these passenger tires in the Federal Motor Vehicle Safety Standards (FMVSS), which are described later in this chapter. All cars are equipped with passenger tires, which usually contain the prefix "P" before their metric size designation molded into the tire sidewall. Even though they are classified as light trucks by the federal government, most SUVs, pickups, and vans used as passenger vehicles are equipped with passenger tires. The kinds of light- and medium-duty trucks used in commercial service, including full-size pickups and vans, have a gross vehicle weight rating of more than 6,000 pounds. These vehicles are usually equipped with tires having the letters "LT" molded into the sidewall. Designed for heavy loads and rough terrain, the LT tires are regulated separately by the federal government and are not part of this study. As a practical matter, the focus is on P-metric tires.

Passenger tires are supplied to automobile manufacturers as original equipment (OE) and to motorists in the replacement market. Statistics on annual shipments of passenger tires for both OE and replacement uses are shown in Figure 2-1. More than 250 million passenger tires were

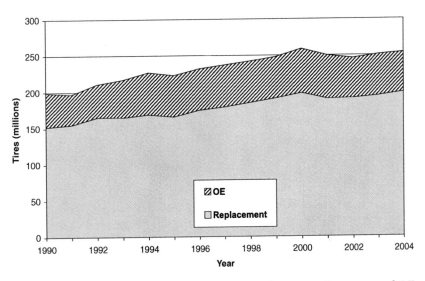

**FIGURE 2-1** Passenger tire shipments in the United States replacement and OE markets, 1990–2004. (Source: RMA 2005, 11–12.)

shipped in the United States in 2004, including about 199 million replacement tires and 53 million OE tires.[1] Thus, replacement tires account for about 80 percent of passenger tire shipments. According to tire dealer data, Americans spent about $20 billion on replacement passenger tires in 2005 (Modern Tire Dealer 2006, 42).

Tire shipment statistics reflect the changing size, age composition, and patterns of use of the U.S. motor vehicle fleet. The number of passenger vehicles in the fleet rose by 21 percent from 1990 to 2002. It was boosted by the addition of 14 million to 17 million new vehicles sold each year and a tendency for vehicles to remain in service longer (Davis and Diegel 2004, 4-5, 4-6). Passenger vehicles are driven an average of 12,000 miles per year, which is an increase of nearly 10 percent since 1990 (Davis and Diegel 2004, 4-2, 4-3). The combination of a growing fleet, vehicles lasting longer, and vehicles being driven more miles has fostered growth in the tire replacement market, which experienced a 33 percent increase in shipments from 1990 to 2004.

## HISTORY OF TIRE DEVELOPMENT

The history of passenger tire development is punctuated by innovations and improvements in tire designs, materials, and manufacturing techniques. Three major periods of development merit attention: (*a*) the early era coinciding with the mass introduction of the automobile from the early 1900s into the 1930s; (*b*) the middle of the 20th century, when synthetic rubber became common and major design innovations such as tubeless and radial-ply tires came about; and (*c*) the period since the mass introduction of radial tires in North America beginning in the 1970s.[2]

---

[1] Data on tire shipments are provided by the Rubber Manufacturers Association (RMA) and do not include shipments by companies that are not members of the association. RMA estimates that 79 million tires were imported in 2004 and that 68 million of them were manufactured by RMA companies (RMA 2005, 18). This differential suggests that about 11 million tires were imported by companies that are not members of RMA. Presumably, most of these 11 million tires were sold in the replacement market. The 11 million are not reflected in Figure 2-1.

[2] Historical information in this section was derived from the following sources: T. French 1989; Tomkins 1981; RMA 2005; M. French 1989; Rajan et al. 1997; Lindemuth 2005; and Moran 2001.

## Early Tire Developments

In the 1840s, Charles Goodyear invented the rubber mixing and curing process known as vulcanization, which was critical in making natural rubber a useful material for a wide range of products. John Boyd Dunlop patented the pneumatic tire for use on bicycles in the 1880s, and by the end of the century, Michelin in France, Goodrich in the United States, and others had adapted the pneumatic tire to the automobile. Within a few years, many companies with now familiar brand names were making tires, including B. F. Goodrich, Firestone, General, Goodyear, and U.S. Rubber (later Uniroyal) in the United States and Continental, Dunlop, Michelin, and Pirelli in Europe.

By World War I, tens of thousands of cars, trucks, and buses were being mass produced each year in the United States, which created a burgeoning demand for tires and many other rubber products such as hoses, belts, and gaskets. New mixers, conveyor systems, and other time- and labor-saving equipment enabled tire production to keep pace with the growing output of automotive assembly lines. Nevertheless, the rapid changes in automobile technologies, new road surfaces, and faster and more frequent driving created new performance demands on tires. In this fast-changing environment, tire companies were forced to learn much about tire design and construction.

Seeking a competitive advantage, tire companies began to invest more in research and development. They found that by replacing the rubber-coated and cross-woven canvas in the tire's casing with plies of rubberized and directionally oriented fabric, the tire's fatigue life was greatly extended. They also found that adding reinforcing agents, such as carbon black powder, to natural rubber greatly increased its resistance to abrasion and allowed tires to operate thousands of miles, rather than hundreds, before wearing out. The discovery of many other valuable rubber additives followed and further extended tire service life by slowing degradation from oxygen, heat, ultraviolet radiation, ozone, and moisture.

The gains in tire wear life were accompanied by gains in operational performance, as understanding grew about the tire's central role in vehicle steering, handling, and braking. Aided by improvements in tire molds and rubber compounding, tire makers introduced better gripping and more durable tread patterns during this period. The bias-ply construction, in which plies are oriented diagonally and at alternating angles, became common. This construction, along with the introduction of the steel rim, allowed the tire to support more weight—and thus enabled cars to become larger and heavier during the 1920s and 1930s.

## Midcentury Developments

When Japan gained control of Asian rubber plantations during World War II, the United States imposed strict controls on rubber consumption by sharply curtailing the production of tires for nonmilitary purposes and by rationing motor fuel and thus driving activity. At the beginning of the war, the federal government estimated that rubber production could be sustained to meet wartime needs for only about 3 years; hence, it called on the nation's chemical companies and research institutions to accelerate the development and introduction of synthetic rubbers made from petroleum and natural gas. This major research and development effort was highly successful and resulted in the annual production of hundreds of thousands of tons of synthetic rubber by 1944.[3]

Having gained experience with synthetics on military tires, tire companies adapted them to passenger tires after the war. When used in tread, synthetic rubber was found to have elasticity characteristics helpful in improving traction. Impermeable synthetic rubbers could be molded into tire inner liners, which allowed the development of tubeless tires. They improved tire puncture resistance by retaining air when damaged and were much easier to mount. By the 1950s, more than two-thirds of the rubber used in tires was synthetic (RMA 2005, 10).

Another important development in tire technology in the decade after World War II was the advent of the steel-belted radial-ply tire and its commercial introduction in Europe by Michelin. Radial-ply tires differed in several respects from bias-ply tires. Whereas the cords in bias-ply tires run diagonally, the carcass cords in radial-ply tires run more directly from bead to bead, perpendicular to the tire's circumference—an orientation made possible because the tread is stabilized by a stiff cir-

---

[3] A history of this period of the tire industry's development is given by Morawetz (2002) and is recounted in the video *Modern Marvels—Rubber* aired by the History Channel and available at www.historychannel.com.

cumferential belt. Today, the belt plies are usually reinforced by small cords made of fine steel cable.

The radial-ply tire offered two critical advantages: a much more stable tread foundation and a more flexible sidewall. These advantages translated into the practical outcomes of longer tread life, better wet and dry traction, improved puncture resistance, and reduced rolling resistance and energy consumption.

## Modern Radial Era

As American motorists began driving foreign vehicles and some U.S. models equipped with radial-ply tires during the 1970s, they began demanding these tires in larger numbers. By the beginning of the 1980s, radial tires had become the standard construction type for both OE and replacement tires. Radials accounted for about 60 percent of passenger tire shipments in 1980, 97 percent by the end of the 1980s, and 99 percent in 2005 (Modern Tire Dealer 2006, 51).

Tire wear life was a key selling point for radials, because average tire wear life increased by thousands of miles. In addition, tire companies marketed "all-season" tires made possible by the stability of the steel belt as a structural foundation, which prevented tread cracking in the required cross-groove pattern for winter traction. This development brought an end to the practice among many North American motorists of switching to specialized snow tires during the winter months.

Radials also offered improved handling, which led to a growing array of tires designed and marketed as "performance," "high performance," and "ultra-high performance." Starting in the 1980s, tire manufacturers started rating more tires in North America according to their designed maximum operating speed. The desired speed rating affected the choice of materials and construction of the tire. For instance, tires with higher speed ratings required stronger steel belts and belt compounds covered by a nylon cap ply. The speed rating letter is printed on the passenger tire's sidewall after sizing information.[4] The most common speed rating

---

[4] The rating is based on laboratory tests during which the tire is pressed against a 1.7-meter-diameter metal drum to reflect its appropriate load and is run at ever-increasing speeds (in 6.2-mph steps in 10-minute increments) until the tire's rated speed is met.

**TABLE 2-1** Common Speed Ratings for U.S. Passenger Tires

| Speed Rating Symbol | Speed (mph) | Speed (km/h) | Example Applications | Percentage of Total OE Tire Shipments in 2004 | Percentage of Total Replacement Tire Shipments in 2004 |
|---|---|---|---|---|---|
| S, T | 112–118 | 180–190 | Family sedans and vans | 83 | 74 |
| H, V | 130–149 | 210–240 | Sport sedans and coupes | 15 | 22 |
| W, Y, Z | >149 | >240 | High-performance sports cars | 2 | 4 |

SOURCE: RMA 2005, 22.

symbols, maximum speeds, and typical applications for U.S. passenger tires are shown in Table 2-1.

While tire manufacturers do not recommend driving at the top speeds for each speed-rated tire, they use the ratings as one means of distinguishing tires with different performance capabilities. In general, tires rated for higher speeds will also be designed to offer superior performance in a number of respects other than speed, such as handling and steering response. The ratings help motorists maintain vehicle speed capability when they replace speed-rated OE tires.

Figure 2-2 displays the information molded in the passenger tire sidewall, including the size designation that usually follows the tire's

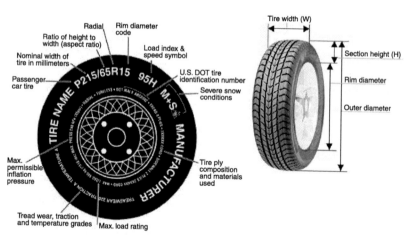

**FIGURE 2-2** Passenger tire sidewall information and major dimensions. (SOURCE: www.tireguides.com.)

name. The tire's section width (in millimeters) is the first number in the size designation, followed by its aspect ratio, which is calculated by dividing the tire's section height by its section width and multiplying by 100. Rim diameter (in inches) is the last number in the series, after "R" for radial. Hence a passenger tire with size designation P215/65/R15 has a section width of 215 millimeters, an aspect ratio (or profile series) of 65, and an inner circumference to fit a rim 15 inches in diameter.

Tire industry survey data indicate that eight of the 10 most popular OE tire sizes for Model Year 2005 passenger vehicles fit 16- and 17-inch rims. Because it takes 3 or more years for OE sizing trends to make their way to the replacement market, tires with 15-inch rim sizes remained common among replacement tires in 2005 (Table 2-2). The OE data in Table 2-2 show the growing popularity of tires with larger section widths and lower aspect ratios—trends that have also become more evident in the replacement market with the availability of "plus-size" custom wheels to replace the original wheel and tire combination.

With regard to possible future trends in the replacement market, tires with specially reinforced sidewalls, known as run-flat tires, have grown in popularity in the OE segment. Although they accounted for less than

**TABLE 2-2**  Passenger Tire Size Popularity, 2005

| OE Tire Size | Percentage of Total OE Tires Shipped | Replacement Tire Size | Percentage of Total Replacement Tires Shipped |
|---|---|---|---|
| P215/60/R16 | 6.0 | P232/60/R16 | 6.4 |
| P205/65/R15 | 5.2 | P235/75/R15 | 6.0 |
| P265/70/R17 | 5.0 | P205/65/R15 | 4.7 |
| P245/65/R17 | 4.6 | P215/70/R15 | 4.0 |
| P235/70/R16 | 4.3 | P205/70/R15 | 3.7 |
| P195/60/R15 | 3.5 | P195/65/R15 | 3.4 |
| P245/70/R17 | 3.2 | P185/65/R14 | 3.1 |
| P205/60/R16 | 3.0 | P195/60/R15 | 2.7 |
| P225/60/R17 | 2.8 | P195/70/R14 | 2.7 |
| P265/65/R17 | 2.6 | P205/55/R16 | 2.4 |
| Total, top 10 | 40.2 | Total, top 10 | 39.1 |

SOURCE: Modern Tire Dealer 2006, 45.

1 percent of replacement sales in 2005, their rate of growth will be influenced by OE acceptance (Modern Tire Dealer 2006, 46). These air-filled but partially structure-supporting tires are designed to operate with the loss of inflation, down to zero inflation pressure for speeds up to 55 mph for a distance of up to 50 miles. Originally developed for two-seat sports cars with little room for spare tires and jacks, run-flat tires can now be found on other passenger vehicles. They are marketed for their convenience and safety in the event of a flat in a remote or hazardous location. As noted later in the report, run-flat tires weigh more than conventional radial tires—which increases their material and production cost—and they tend to exhibit higher rolling resistance.

## TIRE INDUSTRY STRUCTURE

The tire industry is international and driven by competition. The majority of OE and replacement tires sold in the United States are produced by several large domestic and foreign manufacturers, all operating internationally, including Michelin (France), Goodyear (United States), Bridgestone/Firestone (Japan), Pirelli (Italy), Cooper (United States), Toyo (Japan), Kumho (South Korea), Continental (Germany), Hankook (South Korea), Yokohama (Japan), and Sumitomo (Japan). Potentially adding to the competitive mix in the replacement market is the growing number of passenger tires produced by companies based in China, Taiwan, India, and other industrializing countries (Modern Tire Dealer 2006, 51).

Tire manufacturers supply the two distinct—albeit related—markets: OE and replacement. Automobile manufacturers buy in large volumes that give them influence over tire prices and specifications. They demand tires with characteristics that suit their vehicle designs, marketing strategies, and production schedules. In turn, OE orders allow tire companies to keep their production facilities operating at efficient volumes. The OE business also can help generate future sales of replacement tires. By linking its tire lines with a specific vehicle make or model, a tire company can draw on the brand loyalty of motorists. Because four times as many replacement tires as OE tires are sold, such brand loyalty can be valuable to the tire manufacturer.

Like makers of many other consumer goods, tire manufacturers seek to distinguish their products from those of competitors through branding. Most sell under heavily advertised manufacturer (or national "flag") brands as well as associate and specialty brands, some acquired through mergers and acquisitions of well-known tire companies. Goodyear, for instance, sells under its own name and several other nationally recognized brands; it owns Dunlop (in the United States) and Kelly. Likewise, Michelin has acquired the BFGoodrich and Uniroyal brands in the United States, and Bridgestone also sells tires under the Firestone and Dayton brand names. These nine brands accounted for 51.6 percent of the replacement tire consumer market in 2005 (Modern Tire Dealer 2006, 39).

Most major tire companies supply both the OE and the replacement markets. They typically use their flag brands for the former and a combination of flag and associate brands for the latter. An exception to this practice is Cooper Tire, which concentrates on serving the replacement market. It sells tires under its own brand name and under associate brands such as Starfire, Dean, and Mastercraft. In addition, most tire makers supply replacement tires to retailers selling under private labels, such as the Sears Guardsman, Wal-Mart Douglas, and Pep Boys Futura. In these cases, the retailer creates and controls the brand, often contracting for supplies from one or more tire makers offering the lowest price or other valued attributes such as supply reliability.

## OE Market

OE tires outfitted on a specific vehicle are usually developed and supplied by one or two preselected tire makers. From the standpoint of the automobile manufacturer, it can sometimes be advantageous to engage at least two OE tire suppliers to ensure an ample and timely supply and to foster competition. As part of the development process, experimental tires are usually submitted to the automobile manufacturer by the tire maker, along with various test measurements. The tires are evaluated, and further refinements are made as needed. Most automobile companies have in-house tire testing facilities and expertise to assist in tire evaluation and specification.

OE tires are usually specified in both quantitative and qualitative terms. The OE specification sheet will define the tire's physical dimensions, such as mass, width, and diameter within the parameters of tire and rim standards. Because the tire is integral to the vehicle's suspension, steering, acceleration, and braking, the automobile maker will also set precise and quantifiable targets for properties such as force and moment (cornering coefficient, aligning torque coefficient, etc.); deflection (spring rate); and traction (friction coefficients) in wet, dry, and snow conditions. Other quantifiable properties that are usually specified include electrical conductivity (resistance to static shock), speed endurance (suitable to the vehicle's speed capability), tire wear resistance, and rolling resistance (rolling resistance coefficient).[5] In addition, the automobile manufacturer will define several other tire attributes, sometimes through more qualitative means, such as the tire's expected noise and vibration levels, sidewall appearance, and tread image.

Some OE tire specifications are governed by FMVSS such as those covering tire structural safety and rim selection. These apply to all passenger tires. Other OE specifications are strongly influenced by the federal safety standards and other regulations applying to motor vehicles. For example, OE tire designs are influenced by federal standards for passenger vehicle brake systems and motor vehicle fuel economy.

## Replacement Market

The logistics of tire manufacturing, inventorying, and distribution in the replacement market are focused on serving the complete market. Most replacement tires are designed to perform on the wide range of vehicles in the fleet, including vehicle models dating back many years. Hence, whereas the OE market is characterized by the supply of large quantities of select tire types and sizes, suppliers competing in the replacement market must offer a wide variety of tire sizes and types, generally produced in smaller quantities. As a result of market competition, evolving consumer demands and preferences, and changing tire dimensions and specifications introduced in the OE segment, the spectrum of replacement tire sizes and types is continually expanding.

At any one time, replacement tires from hundreds of brands and lines are for sale in the marketplace, which consists of tens of thousands of individual products, or stock-keeping units, when size variability is taken

---

[5] See Lindemuth (2005) for a more detailed listing of performance criteria and measures.

into account. Consumers may choose among a handful to several dozen tire lines for their replacement needs. The choices range from national Internet and mail-order companies to tire dealers, manufacturer outlets, and retail department stores (Figure 2-3). Typically, the tires bought in the replacement market are balanced and mounted by the tire dealer, who adds about $50 to the cost of purchasing a set of four tires (Modern Tire Dealer 2006, 55).

## TIRE SAFETY AND CONSUMER INFORMATION STANDARDS

Even as they market their products to differentiate among tire brands and lines, tire companies recognize the value of standardization. Early

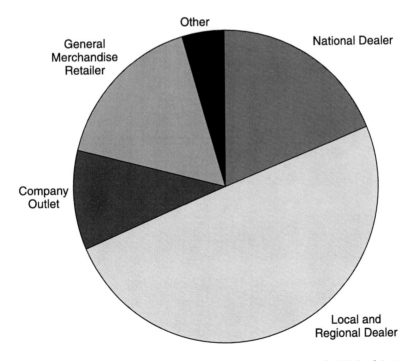

**FIGURE 2-3**  Distribution channels for replacement tires in the United States. (Source: RMA 2005, 13.)

in its history, the tire industry suffered from excessive product differentiation, especially in tire dimensions. Tires designed and configured for just one vehicle proved costly and difficult to replace when damaged or worn. Automobile manufacturers therefore advocated common size designations to promote interchangeability and competition in supply.

Today's passenger tires must conform to a number of standards. Some are required by government, while others are adopted voluntarily by industry and developed through national and international standard-setting bodies. Tire speed ratings, as previously discussed, are an example of a standard developed and implemented by industry. The following subsections describe those standards for passenger tire safety and consumer information that are required by the federal government.[6]

## Federal Safety Regulations for Passenger Tires

Between 1966 and 1970, Congress passed several acts defining and expanding the federal government's role in regulating motor vehicle safety and creating the National Highway Traffic Safety Administration (NHTSA) under the U.S. Department of Transportation to implement them. NHTSA promulgated a series of FMVSS affecting various systems and components of the motor vehicle, such as interior displays and controls, brakes, and occupant protection devices. The rules governing tires cover two main areas: tire structural integrity and fitment.

With regard to structural integrity, the regulations prescribe a battery of tests that must be passed demonstrating

- Tread plunger strength (a round hub is pressed against the tread with a given force to test strength),
- Resistance to bead unseating,
- High-speed performance at constant load and variable speed, and
- Endurance at constant speed and variable load.

After passage of the federal TREAD Act of 2000,[7] a low-pressure tire endurance test was developed for introduction, along with additional

---

[6] See Walter (2005) for a more detailed review of government and industry standards and regulations pertaining to passenger tires.

[7] The Transportation Recall, Enhancement, Accountability, and Documentation (TREAD) Act (Public Law 106-414) was signed into law on November 1, 2000.

requirements for the testing of tire endurance. These requirements are scheduled to take effect in 2007. More additions to the regulations are anticipated in response to the TREAD Act as NHTSA examines tests for tire aging.

With regard to tire sizing and fitment, the federal regulations require that all tires conform to standards for size, load, and pressure relationships developed by standard-setting bodies such as the U.S. Tire and Rim Association, the European Tire and Rim Technical Organization, and the Japan Automobile Tire Manufacturers Association.[8] NHTSA requires tire makers to print sizing information on the tire sidewalls. Tires in compliance with the federal safety standards are marked with the "DOT" symbol (for U.S. Department of Transportation), along with additional information such as the location and date of tire production, maximum pressure, and tire material and construction type.

Other FMVSS regulations influence tire design and construction, including braking standards for motor vehicles. Recently, NHTSA adopted a new rule that will require tire pressure monitoring systems to be installed on all new passenger cars and light trucks starting with 2007 vehicle models.

## Federal Consumer Information Requirements for Passenger Tires

Separate from the federal tire safety requirements are federal requirements intended to provide consumers with information for making tire purchases. The Uniform Tire Quality Grading (UTQG) system applies to all passenger tires with the exception of winter tires and compact spares. In its current form since 1980, the UTQG system consists of grades for tread wear, wet traction, and temperature resistance. Manufacturers typically test one or more tire models from a tire line or grouping to establish the grades for each of the three qualities, which are then molded on the tire sidewall.

---

[8] Other bodies include the Deutsche Industrie Norm, the British Standards Institution, the Scandinavian Tire and Rim Organization, and the Tyre and Rim Association of Australia.

### Tread Wear Grade

The UTQG tread wear grade is a comparative rating generated from the results of an outdoor highway test course in which the subject tire is run in a convoy with several standardized "course-monitoring" tires. After 7,200 miles, the subject tire's wear rate is compared with that of the monitoring tires. The tire manufacturer assigns a tread wear grade on the basis of extrapolations of measured wear rates. The ranking scheme suggests that a tire rated 200 should wear twice as long as a tire rated 100 on the government test course. The relative performance of tires, however, depends on the conditions of use, and therefore it may depart significantly from the norm because of variations in operating conditions and maintenance. The 2,371 rated passenger tire lines have the following distribution of tread wear grades according to information on NHTSA's website:[9] 200 or lower, 11 percent; 201 to 300, 21 percent; 301 to 400, 33 percent; 401 to 500, 22 percent; 501 to 600, 8 percent; above 600, 5 percent.

Neither NHTSA nor tire manufacturers are willing to associate expected mileage levels with particular grades because of the variability in wear that can occur on the basis of vehicle operating conditions, road conditions, tire maintenance, and individual driving patterns.

### Traction Grade

UTQG traction grades are based on a tire's measured coefficient of friction when it is tested on wet asphalt and concrete surfaces. The subject tire is placed on an instrumented axle of a skid trailer, which is pulled behind a truck at 50 mph on wet asphalt and concrete surfaces. The trailer's brakes are momentarily locked, and sensors on the axle measure the longitudinal braking forces as it slides in a straight line. The coefficient of friction is then determined as the ratio of this sliding forced to the tire load. Grades of AA, A, B, and C are assigned according to the criteria shown in Table 2-3.

Traction grades are intended to indicate a tire's ability to stop on wet pavement. The UTQG traction grade does not take into account other aspects of traction, such as peak traction, traction on dry or snow-covered surfaces, or cornering traction. NHTSA website data indicate that of the

---

[9] www.safercar.gov/tires/pages/Tires2.cfm. Results reported to NHTSA are not sales weighted.

**TABLE 2-3**  UTQG Traction Grades

| Traction Grade | Wet Asphalt Sliding Friction Coefficient | Wet Concrete Sliding Friction Coefficient |
|---|---|---|
| AA | >0.54 | >0.38 |
| A | >0.47 | >0.35 |
| B | >0.38 | >0.26 |
| C | <0.38 | <0.26 |

2,371 rated passenger tire lines, 4 percent were graded AA, 78 percent A, and 18 percent B and C.[10]

### Temperature Grade

A tire operating at normal speeds can achieve internal temperatures in excess of 180°F. The UTQG temperature grade indicates the tire's resistance to the generation of heat during operation at elevated speeds. Sustained high temperature can cause the material of the tire to degrade and reduce tire life, while excessive temperature can lead to sudden tire failure. Tires are tested under controlled conditions on a high-speed laboratory test wheel. The focus is on speed effects of properly loaded and inflated tires. Underinflation and overloading, which can cause heat buildup at normal speeds, are not tested. Tires are rated A, B, or C, with A being the highest grade. Tires graded A completed a 30-minute run at 115 mph without failing; tires graded B completed a 30-minute run at 100 mph, but not 115 mph; and tires graded C failed to complete a 30-minute run at 100 mph. According to NHTSA website data, 27 percent of the 2,371 rated passenger tire lines have an A grade, 59 percent a B grade, and 11 percent a C grade.[11]

## SUMMARY

Most vehicles used for personal and family transportation, including the growing number of vehicles designated as light trucks and multi-purpose passenger vehicles (i.e., vans, SUVs), are equipped with tires

---

[10] www.safercar.gov/Tires/pages/Tires2.cfm. The data are undated.
[11] www.safercar.gov/tires/pages/TireRatTemperature.htm. The data are undated.

that are regulated by the federal government as passenger tires. Passenger tires make up the large majority of OE and replacement tires in the light motor vehicle fleet.

Today's passenger tire is a complex engineering composite that has evolved over the past century to function as a crucial structural and dynamic component of the vehicle. Its main structural components, as in all pneumatic tires, are the casing, tread, and bead. All of the components have been the subject of major advances in designs, materials, and construction methods. The most significant development in recent decades was the mass introduction of radial-ply tires starting in the 1970s in the United States. The radial-ply construction has had substantial positive effects on the durability, handling, and energy performance of passenger tires.

About 250 million tires are shipped each year in the United States, and about 80 percent are replacement tires. The number and type of tires shipped reflect the size and composition of the passenger vehicle fleet. Growing sales of light trucks (vans, pickups, and SUVs) have led to an expanding array of sizes and performance capabilities in OE tires, which have evolved in the replacement market.

The tire industry serves two distinct, albeit related, markets: OE and replacement. OE tires are developed for specific vehicles and are designed to work closely with the vehicle's suspension, steering, and braking systems and to meet other automobile maker goals for their tires such as appearance, noise, durability, and rolling resistance. Replacement tires, in contrast, are designed to perform on a much wider range of vehicle brands and models. Variations in tire sizes, models, and types, as well as required years of availability, mean that there are tens of thousands of unique replacement tire products in the marketplace.

Passenger tires must conform to a number of government and industry standards. All passenger tires must pass federal tests for structural integrity, which are aimed at preventing rapid loss of pressure, unseating, and loss of structural form that could cause a driver to lose control of the vehicle. In consumer-oriented regulations separate from its safety requirements, the federal government also requires passenger tires to be graded for traction, tread wear, and temperature resistance. The grades, which are molded into the tire sidewall, are not safety minima but are intended to provide consumers with information for making tire purchases. The tire industry has established its own standards for tire sizing and fitting and for rating a tire's speed capabilities, which are also used by consumers in selecting tires suited to their particular vehicles and driving patterns.

## REFERENCES

*Abbreviation*

RMA     Rubber Manufacturers Association

Davis, S. C., and S. W. Diegel. 2004. *Transportation Energy Data Book: Edition 24.* Report ORNL-6973. Center for Transportation Analysis, Oak Ridge National Laboratory, Oak Ridge, Tenn.

French, M. 1989. Manufacturing and Marketing: Vertical Integration in the U.S. Tire Manufacturing Industry, 1890s–1980s. *Business and Economic History,* Vol. 18, pp. 178–187.

French, T. 1989. *Tyre Technology.* Adam Hilger, Bristol, England.

Lindemuth, B. E. 2005. An Overview of Tire Technology. In *The Pneumatic Tire* (J. D. Walter and A. N. Gent, eds.), National Highway Traffic Safety Administration, Washington, D.C., pp. 1–27.

Modern Tire Dealer. 2006. *Modern Tire Dealer's Facts Issue.* www.moderntiredealer.com. Jan.

Moran, T. 2001. The Radial Revolution. *Invention and Technology,* Spring, pp. 28–39.

Morawetz, H. 2002. *Polymers: The Origin and Growth of a Science.* Dover Phoenix Editions, New York.

Rajan, R., P. Volpin, and L. Zingales. 1997. The Eclipse of the U.S. Tire Industry. Working paper, National Bureau of Economic Research Conference on Mergers and Productivity, March.

RMA. 2005. *Factbook 2005: U.S. Tire Shipment Activity Report for Statistical Year 2004.* Washington, D.C.

Tomkins, E. S. 1981. *The History of the Pneumatic Tyre.* Eastland Press, London.

Walter, J. D. 2005. Tire Standards and Specifications. In *The Pneumatic Tire* (J. D. Walter and A. N. Gent, eds.), National Highway Traffic Safety Administration, Washington, D.C., pp. 655–669.

# 3

# The Tire's Influence on Passenger Vehicle Fuel Consumption

In every important respect, the quality and performance of today's passenger tires are superior to those of their predecessors. Tires wear longer, are more resistant to damage, handle and track better, and are easier to maintain. Each generation of tire engineers has sought to balance these and other performance characteristics, commensurate with technology cost and capabilities, government regulations, consumer demands, and operational requirements.

In requesting this study, Congress did not give specific reasons for its interest in tire energy performance. However, it did ask for estimates of the fuel savings associated with low-rolling-resistance tires. Accordingly, the committee construed its charge to focus on the contribution of tires to passenger vehicle fuel consumption, as opposed to all energy flows during a tire's life cycle, from the energy used in raw materials and manufacturing processes to recycling and disposal. While a full accounting of such life-cycle effects is relevant for policy making, it would have exceeded the scope and capabilities of this study.

The chapter begins with a review of the history of interest in vehicle fuel economy and the effect of tires on fuel consumption. Rolling resistance, which is the main source of the tire's influence on fuel consumption, is then explained. Over the past 25 years, several data sets containing measurements of the rolling resistance characteristics of new tires have been made available to the public. These data sets are examined. Although they are limited in coverage, they offer insights into changes in rolling resistance over time and the implications for passenger vehicle fuel economy.

## RECENT HISTORY OF INTEREST
## IN VEHICLE FUEL ECONOMY

Fuel economy is typically expressed as the average number of miles a vehicle travels per gallon of motor fuel, usually as miles per gallon (mpg). The interest of both consumers and government in fuel economy was galvanized during the mid-1970s in response to escalating fuel prices prompted by the oil embargo of the Organization of Petroleum Exporting Countries. At that time, new cars sold in the United States averaged less than 16 mpg. As gasoline prices jumped by more than 25 percent within months, motorists and policy makers focused their attention on energy conservation for the first time since World War II. During the decade that followed—which included further jumps in gasoline and diesel fuel prices—the average fuel economy of new vehicles grew by more than 50 percent (NRC 1992, 14). During this period some policy makers also began to focus on the role of motor fuel in the atmospheric buildup of carbon dioxide and other greenhouse gases. The buildup threatened climate change and provided further impetus for improvements in fuel economy (TRB 1997).

A number of policies aimed at energy conservation were pursued starting in the mid-1970s. Congress passed the national 55-mph speed limit in 1974. A year later, it instructed the U.S. Environmental Protection Agency (EPA) to require the posting of fuel economy labels (window stickers) on all new vehicles for sale. The U.S. Department of Energy was charged with developing and publicizing an annual fuel economy mileage guide. The federal "gas guzzler" excise tax, which raised the price of automobiles with low fuel economy, was introduced in 1979. Perhaps the most significant program originating from that period was the corporate average fuel economy (CAFE) program.[1] For the first time, Congress established fuel economy standards for passenger cars and light trucks. The program, administered by the National Highway Traffic Safety Administration (NHTSA), mandated a sales-weighted average fuel economy for different vehicle categories produced by all automobile manufacturers. Each vehicle's rating would be determined by EPA's city

---

[1] CAFE was enacted as part of the Energy Policy Conservation Act of 1975.

and highway driving tests developed originally for emissions testing and certification.[2]

There are various ways to increase vehicle fuel economy. Among them are reducing the loads that must be overcome by the vehicle and increasing the efficiency of its engine, its transmission, and other components that generate and transfer power to the axles. Since the 1970s, the emphasis given to specific means has fluctuated in response to regulation, market forces, and technology cost and capabilities. At first, automobile manufacturers focused on reducing vehicle mass, most commonly by moving to smaller vehicles constructed of lighter materials (NRC 1992). By the 1980s, the emphasis shifted to increasing engine and transmission efficiency and reducing other vehicle loads such as aerodynamic drag and the power demanded by accessories (NRC 1992). By the end of the 1980s, however, fuel economy gains in passenger cars and light trucks had flattened out. At the same time, gasoline prices had fallen back and public demand for fuel economy waned (NRC 1992, 17).

While modest additional improvements in fuel economy were made during the 1990s, the average fuel economy of the passenger vehicle fleet had already peaked. As larger and more powerful vehicles came back in demand, the modest fuel economy improvements that did occur were achieved by changes in vehicle features not affecting vehicle size or interior space, such as accessories, construction materials, lubricants, and tires. Continuing improvements in engine efficiency were also sought to maintain fuel economy as the market shifted to larger and more powerful vehicles.

Most recently, in a period characterized by higher gasoline prices, mounting concern over national security, and growing consumer interest in fuel economy, NHTSA has set light truck standards to increase at about 0.5 mpg per year from 2005 through 2011. Passenger car standards have not been changed. It is notable, however, that NHTSA and EPA are revising the long-standing means of measuring and calculating vehicle fuel economy, which could eventually affect the implementation of CAFE.

---

[2] EPA is responsible for providing fuel economy data that are posted on the window stickers of new vehicles. Fuel economy data are also used by the U.S. Department of Energy to publish the annual *Fuel Economy Guide*, by the U.S. Department of Transportation to administer CAFE, and by the Internal Revenue Service to collect gas guzzler taxes.

# EXAMINING THE INFLUENCE OF TIRES ON VEHICLE FUEL ECONOMY

The advent of CAFE and other government policies to promote fuel economy prompted automobile manufacturers and engineers to take a closer look at the many factors influencing vehicle fuel consumption. While explanations of these influences are available elsewhere (Schuring 1980; Ross 1997; NRC 2002; Sovran and Blaser 2003), a general overview is helpful in understanding the contribution of tires to energy consumption.

The amount of fuel consumed by a motor vehicle over a distance is affected by the efficiency of the vehicle in converting the chemical energy in motor fuel into mechanical energy and transmitting it to the axles to drive the wheels. Figure 3-1 depicts the energy flows and sinks for a conventional gasoline-powered midsize passenger car. Most of the energy available in the fuel tank—about two-thirds—is lost in converting heat into mechanical work at the engine, much of it unavoidably. For urban trips consisting of stop-and-go driving, a significant percentage (about 15 to 20 percent) is also lost in standby operations during coasting, braking, and idling in traffic. For urban driving, only 10 to 15 percent of the fuel energy is ultimately transmitted as power to the wheels. Because standby losses are lower during highway driving and because the engine is operating more efficiently, a higher percentage of fuel energy—about 20 percent—makes its way to the wheels. While the specific percentages will vary by vehicle type and trip, the flows shown in Figure 3-1 are generally representative of passenger vehicles today.

For both urban and highway driving, the mechanical energy that does make its way through the driveline to turn the wheels is consumed by three sinks: aerodynamic drag, rolling resistance, and braking. Braking consumes momentum from the vehicle, which must be replenished by acceleration. Because frequent stopping and starting entail repeated braking and acceleration, braking is a major consumer of mechanical energy during urban driving. In contrast, aerodynamic drag consumes relatively more energy during highway driving since this resistive force escalates with vehicle speed.

In comparison, the energy losses from rolling resistance (for a given vehicle and set of tires) are mainly a function of miles traveled. For reasons explained later in this chapter, vehicle speed has a limited effect on

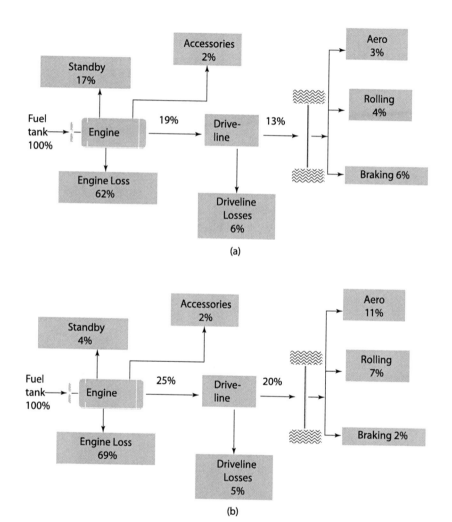

**FIGURE 3-1** Example energy flows for a late-model midsize passenger car: (*a*) urban driving; (*b*) highway driving. [SOURCE: U.S. Department of Energy (www.fueleconomy.gov/feg/atv.shtml).]

rolling resistance except at the highest speeds reached on occasion during highway driving. As a result, the energy lost per mile because of rolling resistance will be similar for a given vehicle and set of tires over a wide range of urban or highway driving cycles. While the percentage contribution of rolling resistance to total energy consumed per mile depends on the contribution of other sinks, its absolute contribution does not.

In sum, for most conventional motor vehicles in common use, the majority of the energy contained in motor fuel is dissipated as unrecoverable heat from engine combustion and friction in the engine, driveline, axles, and wheel bearings. Some of the energy output from the engine is used during idling and to power vehicle accessories. Only about 12 to 20 percent of the energy originating in the fuel tank is ultimately transmitted through the vehicle's driveline as mechanical energy to turn the wheels. Rolling resistance consumes about one-third of this mechanical energy output. Rolling resistance, therefore, directly consumes a small portion (4 to 7 percent) of the total energy expended by the vehicle. However, reducing rolling resistance, and thus reducing mechanical energy demand, by a given amount will translate into a larger reduction in total fuel consumption because less fuel energy will need to be sent to the engine in the first place. The effect on total fuel consumption will depend on a number of factors, including the efficiency of the engine and driveline as well as the amount of energy used by accessories.

As explained later in this chapter, for most passenger vehicles, a 10 percent reduction in rolling resistance will lead to a 1 to 2 percent increase in fuel economy and a proportional reduction in fuel consumption. This assumes that other influences on fuel consumption are held constant, especially miles of travel. As a practical matter, total travel by the U.S. passenger vehicle fleet continually increases; it has grown by an average of 1 or 2 percent annually during the past several decades. Accordingly, the time frame over which the change in fuel economy occurs—in the near term or over a longer period—is important in calculating the national fuel savings. A related issue is that improvements in vehicle fuel economy have the secondary effect of increasing vehicle travel. As vehicle fuel economy improves, the per-mile cost of driving is effectively lowered, which may spur some additional driving and fuel consumption. This response, known as the rebound effect, is usually considered in evaluations of CAFE and other fuel economy programs. After examining the literature, Small and Van Dender (2005) estimate that 2 to 11 percent of the expected fuel savings from a fuel economy improvement is offset by increased driving. While this second-order effect is recognized again later in the report, the calculations of fuel savings do not account for it. For simplicity, it is assumed that miles traveled are unchanged.

Estimates of consumer fuel savings from reductions in rolling resistance are made in Chapter 5. The focus of the remainder of this chapter is on describing the factors causing and influencing rolling resistance as well as the properties of today's passenger tires with respect to this characteristic.

## FACTORS CAUSING AND INFLUENCING ROLLING RESISTANCE

### General Information

Short of changing the characteristics of the road surface, there are two main ways to minimize rolling resistance. One is to drive on properly inflated and aligned tires. The other is to use tires that possess low rolling resistance at proper inflation levels. Maintaining proper tire inflation and alignment is important for motor vehicle safety as well as for fuel economy; this is true for all pneumatic tires regardless of their design. This section therefore focuses on designing tires with lower rolling resistance when properly inflated.[3]

It has long been known that a rolling tire must be supplied energy continuously in order to avoid losing speed. Until the 1970s, however, understanding the causes of tire rolling resistance drew little interest (Schuring 1980). Only a few dozen technical papers had been published on the subject, and no standard methods were in place for measuring tire rolling resistance characteristics (Clark 1983). Rising energy prices during the 1970s prompted more concerted efforts to highlight the causes of rolling resistance and the effects of specific tire construction properties on this characteristic.

---

[3] See LaClair (2005) for a recent and thorough review and explanation of the technical literature on rolling resistance.

With the aid of advances in analytical and experimental capabilities, such as thermography and finite element modeling, tires were examined for a wide range of design, operating, and environmental conditions that could affect rolling resistance. Consideration was given to the effect of tire dimensions, construction types, and materials; load and inflation pressures; wheel alignment; steering and torque inputs; vehicle operating speeds; and ambient temperatures (Clark and Dodge 1978; Schuring 1980).[4] Even the contributions of roadway surface types and textures were examined (DeRaad 1978; Velinsky and White 1979).

Because of this research, much more is known and documented today about the sources of rolling resistance and their interacting effects.

## Role of Hysteresis

Pneumatic tires offer a number of advantages related to the highly compliant nature of rubber. The rubber tire interacts with the hard road surface by deforming under load, thereby generating the forces responsible for traction, cornering, acceleration, and braking. It also provides increased cushioning for ride comfort. A disadvantage, however, is that energy is expended as the pneumatic tire repeatedly deforms and recovers during its rotation under the weight of the vehicle.

Most of this energy loss stems from the viscoelastic behavior of rubber materials. Rubber exhibits a combination of viscous and elastic behavior. A purely elastic material is one in which all energy stored in the material during loading is returned when the load is removed and the material quickly recovers its shape. A purely viscous material, on the other hand, stores no strain energy, and all of the energy required to deform the material is simultaneously converted into heat. In the case of a viscoelastic material, some of the energy stored is recovered upon removal of the load, while the rest is converted to heat. The mechanical energy loss associated with each cycle of deformation and recovery is known as hysteresis.[5]

---

[4] Mars and Luchini (1999) provide an overview of this work.
[5] Hysteresis also occurs because of deflection of the road surface. On paved surfaces that deflect very little under the loads of passenger cars, tire deformation is the main source of hysteresis.

### Tire Design and Hysteresis

The characteristics affecting hysteresis are a tire's design and construction and the material types and quantities used.

The beneficial effect of radial-ply constructions in reducing tire rolling resistance is an example of the influence of tire construction on hysteresis. In comparison with the bias-ply tire, the steel-belted radial tire reduced the deformation of the tread in the contact patch. Hence, in addition to affecting tire handling, endurance, and ride comfort, the changeover from bias-ply to radial-ply tires during the 1970s and 1980s reduced tire rolling resistance by an estimated 25 percent without requiring major changes in the polymers used (Schuring 1980, 601).

There are several measures of the geometry of a tire, including its outer diameter, rim diameter, and width. Reducing a tire's aspect ratio—that is, its section height relative to its section width—should reduce hysteresis if it is accomplished by shortening and stiffening of the sidewalls. The aspect ratio, however, can be altered in other ways—for instance, by changing the tire's outer diameter, width, rim diameter, or all three dimensions. Moreover, changing tire geometry is difficult without changing other characteristics of the tire that influence hysteresis, such as mass, material types, and construction features. As a result, it can be difficult to know, a priori, how specific changes in tire dimensions will translate to changes in rolling resistance (Schuring 1980; Chang and Shackelton 1983; Schuring and Futamura 1990; Pillai and Fielding-Russell 1991).

Because hysteresis is fundamentally related to the viscoelastic deformation of the rubber used in tire construction, changes in material formulations and quantities affect rolling resistance. While reducing the amount of hysteretic material in any component of the tire might appear to be a straightforward way to reduce rolling resistance, different components must contain different amounts and types of hysteretic material. In particular, the tread contains much of the hysteretic material in the tire. Not only is the tread made of rubber compounds that are designed to improve wet traction, the tread band also contains relatively large quantities of material to prolong wear life. Studies indicate that the tread alone can contribute more than half of hysteretic energy losses in a tire (Chang and Shackelton 1983; Martini 1983; LaClair 2005).

Related to the effect of tread mass and volume on hysteresis is the effect of tread wear on rolling resistance. As tread depth (that is, the depth of grooves in the tread pattern) diminishes with wear, a tire loses about 15 percent of its mass—since the tread band typically accounts for about one-quarter of a tire's weight. The moderating effect of tread wear on rolling resistance has been examined and quantified to some extent. Martini (1983) compared the tire rolling resistance occurring when the tread was new (100 percent) with that occurring when the tire was buffed to various stages of wear (75, 50, 25, and 0 percent remaining tread). These experiments suggested that rolling resistance declined by 26 percent over the entire wear life. After reviewing many similar experimental studies conducted before 1980, Schuring (1980, 683–684) concluded that rolling resistance declined by an average of about 20 percent over the tread life, dependent on design details.

The tread compound consists of rubbers that contain different polymers, reinforcing fillers, extender oils, antidegradants, and other materials. Their effect on rolling resistance can be significant but complex. Compounding material formulas are developed with many requirements and performance properties in mind. Therefore, these formulas tend to be proprietary, and the rolling resistance effects of different materials and their interactions are difficult to study. The type of rubber used influences rolling resistance; notably, synthetic rubbers tend to exhibit greater rolling resistance than natural rubbers. The reinforcing fillers in the compound, which are essential for abrasion resistance, also affect rolling resistance. Carbon black is the most widely used filler. During the early 1990s, Michelin introduced a silica filler in conjunction with a silane coupling agent as a means of reducing rolling resistance while retaining wet traction characteristics. Although carbon black remains the predominant filler, all major tire companies have reportedly constructed tires containing silica–silane and carbon black in the tread compound. This technology, initially promoted as a breakthrough in the ability to balance rolling resistance with other tire performance properties, is examined in more detail in Chapter 5.

### Tire Operating Variables and Hysteresis

A number of tire operating conditions affect rolling resistance. The most important are load, inflation pressure, and temperature. Tires operated at the top speeds associated with normal highway driving may exhibit increases in rolling resistance as the frequency of tire deformation increases. However, as speed increases, the tire's internal temperature rises, offsetting some of the increased rolling resistance. The net effect is that operating speed tends to have a small influence on rolling resistance compared with that of many other operating variables under normal driving conditions (Schuring 1980, 638; Schuring and Futamura 1990, 351; Chang and Shackelton 1983, 19; Hall and Moreland 2001, 530; LaClair 2005, 491). Another nontire operating condition, the road surface, can have an appreciable effect on rolling resistance, as discussed briefly later.

The more a tire at a given pressure is loaded, the more it deforms; hence, hysteresis increases with wheel load. Indeed, the relationship between rolling resistance and sidewall deflection due to load is approximately linear, so increasing the load on a tire results in a near-proportional increase in total rolling resistance. As described later, this linear relationship allows rolling resistance to be expressed as a coefficient with respect to load under normal operating conditions.

Inflation pressure affects tire deformation. Tires with reduced inflation exhibit more sidewall bending and tread shearing. The relationship between rolling resistance and pressure is not linear, but it is consistent enough for rules of thumb to be applied. Schuring (1980) observes that for conventional passenger tires, an increase in inflation pressure from 24 to 29 pounds per square inch (psi) will reduce rolling resistance by 10 percent. For a tire inflated to pressures between 24 and 36 psi, each drop of 1 psi leads to a 1.4 percent increase in its rolling resistance. The response is even greater for pressure changes below 24 psi. Maintenance of tire pressure is therefore important in preventing excessive deformation and hysteresis, as well as in achieving intended wear, traction, handling, and structural performance.

The temperature of a tire is affected by ambient conditions, tire design and materials, running time, and speed. Higher ambient temperatures are associated with reduced rolling resistance because the amount of energy dissipated when the rubber is subjected to repeated deformation declines moderately as temperature rises, which is a commonly observed behavior of viscoelastic materials. Accordingly, the length of time a tire has been running since the last cool-off affects rolling resistance, which declines until the passenger tire has been rolling for about 30 minutes.

At that point an equilibrium temperature is reached and rolling resistance stabilizes.

### Road Surface and Hysteresis

Researchers have known for some time that rough road surfaces contribute to rolling loss by exacerbating tire deformation. This effect can increase energy losses by 5 to 20 percent (Velinsky and White 1979; DeRaad 1978). Road roughness has two components: macrotexture and microtexture. The first relates mainly to the surface condition on a scale of inches to feet and reflects the presence of cracks, ruts, bumps, and other surface irregularities. Macrotexture can include intentional changes in surface texture, such as surface grooving to improve water runoff. The second component, microtexture, relates to smaller-scale asperities in the road surface that are millimeters or even fractions of a millimeter in size and reflect the coarseness of the surface texture. Tires operated on a rough macrotexture or rough microtexture will deform more and suffer greater energy loss. They will also experience faster tread wear.

The roadway can also contribute to rolling resistance by deflecting or deforming under the weight of the wheel load. How much energy is lost will depend on the rigidity of the roadbed and overlay. Dirt and gravel roads deform the most and give rise to twice as much rolling resistance as harder paved surfaces (DeRaad 1978). However, most driving occurs on paved surfaces, which can vary in rigidity depending on the overlay, base, and subgrade. The most rigid, or nondeformable, pavements tend to be those with a concrete surface layer and reinforced base, followed by an asphalt surface on a concrete base, and an asphalt surface on a compacted gravel or soil base. The rigidity of asphalt overlay depends on the amount and type of asphalt used in relation to aggregate and on environmental conditions such as temperature. A rubber-modified asphalt overlay (often derived from the ground rubber of scrap tires) will deform more under load and thus should create more rolling resistance than harder asphalt pavements.

## MEASURING AND EXPRESSING ROLLING RESISTANCE

The fact that rolling resistance relates linearly to wheel load allows it to be expressed as a near-constant coefficient relative to wheel load. The rolling resistance coefficient (RRC), referred to extensively throughout the remainder of this report, is derived by dividing rolling resistance by wheel load. It is typically measured for new tires—as is the case for many of the data presented in the remainder of this report—but can be measured at any point in a tire's lifetime. For most passenger tires sold in the United States, the coefficient of the tire measured when it is new falls between 0.007 and 0.014. Hence, for a tire in this range under a load of 1,000 pounds, the rolling resistance is 7 to 14 pounds, resulting in 28 to 56 pounds of total force for the four tires on a vehicle weighing 4,000 pounds, including passenger and cargo load. At 60 mph, a total rolling resistance of 40 pounds consumes about 7 horsepower.

The Society of Automotive Engineers (SAE) has established two standard procedures for measuring tire rolling resistance. Because the procedures, J1269 and J2452, are both laboratory tests, they allow for repeatability and instrumentation accuracy as well as controls for operating conditions and other exogenous influences. They are described in detail in the Appendix. What distinguishes the two test procedures the most is that the first measures rolling resistance at a single speed (50 mph), while the latter measures it over a range of speeds. J1269 was developed to assist tire engineers in quantifying rolling resistance in a consistent way to allow for the more precise balancing of this tire property with other quantifiable properties, such as cornering, traction, and heat generation. J2452 was developed later to provide additional quantification of a tire's rolling resistance for more precise inputs to the driving cycles used for federal vehicle emissions and fuel economy regulatory compliance. The speed-adjusted measurements generated from J2452 can be entered into simulated driving cycles, such as those used for testing new vehicles for CAFE compliance.

By providing established and commonly accepted methods for measuring tire rolling resistance, the SAE procedures allow reliable comparisons of tires. Of course, neither procedure can take into account all the conditions an individual tire will experience under varied driving and operating conditions over tens of thousands of miles. Variations in road surfaces, inflation pressures, wheel maintenance and alignment, and other conditions will affect rolling resistance in the field. All of these factors— as well as limited correlation of testing equipment—will lead to some discrepancies among individual laboratory measurements and between laboratory results and field experience.

For the most part, the SAE tests are performed only on new tires, and thus they offer little insight into how individual tires experience changing rolling resistance as they are used, wear, and age.[6] As will be discussed in more detail later, the absence of rolling resistance data for tires at different stages of their use makes it difficult to calculate average rolling resistance and thus to know precisely how one tire's lifetime energy performance will differ from that of another.

## ROLLING RESISTANCE AND FUEL ECONOMY

Knowledge of a tire's RRC allows calculations of its effect on vehicle fuel economy. Such calculations have been the subject of empirical models, laboratory experiments, and road measurements for many years. General approximations, or rules of thumb, of the fuel economy effects of incremental changes in tire rolling resistance have been developed. The most common way to describe this relationship is by relating the percentage change in RRC to the percentage change in fuel economy; for example, "a 10 percent change in RRC yields a 2 percent change in vehicle fuel economy." This approach is generally acceptable for the relatively narrow range of RRCs observed for most passenger tires. However, it can introduce imprecision, since a given percentage change in fuel economy is linearly related to an *absolute* change in rolling resistance. As RRC becomes smaller, a given percentage reduction in RRC tends to have a diminished effect on fuel economy. Nevertheless, because percentage change is a common and widely understood concept, it is often used in this report. Many studies have examined the relationship between rolling resistance and fuel economy. A comprehensive review of fuel economy data from more than a dozen studies published before 1990 was undertaken by Schuring and Futamura (1990). The authors found a narrow range of results that suggested an approximately linear relationship between changes in rolling resistance and fuel economy. During the time period of the studies reviewed, new-tire RRCs were seldom lower than 0.01, so that a 10 percent differential was equivalent to a difference in

---

[6] The SAE tests can be performed on used tires. Apart from limited demand for such testing, a main difficulty is obtaining large numbers of tires with definable and realistic wear conditions that can be replicated.

RRC of 0.001 or more. For passenger cars operated in urban environments characterized by stop-and-go driving, a 10 percent reduction in the average RRC for all tires on a vehicle was found to increase fuel economy by 1.2 to 1.5 percent. For highway driving characterized by higher and more consistent travel speeds, the same percentage reduction in RRC increased fuel economy by 0.9 to 2.1 percent. Estimates of the fuel economy response for combined urban and highway driving schedules varied from 1.15 to 2.1 percent per 10 percent change in RRC. While fewer studies were performed on light-duty trucks, their corresponding fuel economy effects ranged from 0.95 to 1.25 percent for combined urban and highway driving.

The findings of Schuring and Futamura were consistent with common assumptions and rules of thumb concerning the fuel economy response to changes in rolling resistance. For instance, Thompson and Reineman (1981), in assisting EPA with the development of fuel economy models, assumed that a change of 0.001 in RRC would change vehicle fuel consumption by 1 percent during urban driving and 2 percent during highway driving. Studies published more recently have yielded similar results. Schuring (1994) estimated that for passenger tires having an RRC of 0.012, a 10 percent reduction in RRC will cause fuel economy to increase by 1.4 percent on average—and within a range of 0.7 to 2 percent, depending on the tire's duty cycle and operating conditions. Schuring found the relationship to be approximately linear. He calculated that the theoretical limit for fuel savings—that is, under the hypothesis that rolling resistance could be eliminated entirely—is 14 percent for conventional passenger cars and 28 percent for fully loaded large trucks. More recently, Hall and Moreland (2001, 527) assumed a more conservative 0.5 to 1.5 percent increase in fuel economy per 10 percent reduction in RRC, although they did not give the baseline RRC.

In interviews with original equipment manufacturers (OEMs) for this study (as discussed in more detail later in the chapter), one—General Motors—permitted the use of its CAFE simulation model to predict fuel consumption effects from changes in RRC. The committee commissioned Environmental Energy Analysis, Inc. (EEA), to run and review the simulations, including the fuel economy model of the National Energy Technology Laboratory (NETL). In addition, Professor Marc Ross of the

**TABLE 3-1**  Percentage Change in Fuel Economy (Miles per Gallon) in Response to a 10 percent Change in Tire Rolling Resistance Under Several Simulation Models (Assumed Baseline RRC = 0.008)

| Simulation Model | 10% Decrease in RRC to 0.0072 | | 10% Increase in RRC to 0.0088 | |
|---|---|---|---|---|
| | City | Highway | City | Highway |
| GM | 1.08 | 1.60 | −1.44 | −1.87 |
| NETL | 0.70 | 1.95 | −0.67 | −1.72 |
| Ross | 0.95 | 1.86 | −0.95 | −1.86 |
| EEA | 1.28 | 1.96 | −1.27 | −1.91 |

NOTE: The modeled vehicle is a midsize, four-cylinder passenger car. Confidence intervals for the simulation results were not available.

University of Michigan provided the study committee with estimates of the fuel consumption effects derived from a computational model. All of the models are based on a four-cylinder, gasoline-powered midsize passenger car. The results of the simulations are given in Table 3-1. They too assume a 10 percent change in RRC, but from a conservatively smaller base coefficient of 0.008—meaning an incremental change in RRC of ±0.0008.

The results of literature reviews and the output of these simulations are sufficiently consistent to estimate a response range for RRC that is meaningful for most driving patterns and common types of passenger vehicles. They are consistent with the long-standing rule of thumb that a 10 percent reduction in RRC will yield a 1 to 2 percent increase in vehicle fuel economy. The lower end of the 1 to 2 percent range, however, is more relevant for tires having low RRCs and driven in urban environments, while the higher end is more relevant for tires having higher RRCs and driven on highways. As explained above, each percentage reduction in RRC becomes smaller in absolute terms. Hence, a more precise way to state the fuel economy response is that each 0.001 reduction in RRC causes fuel economy to increase by 1 to 2 percent.

## ROLLING RESISTANCE DATA FOR PASSENGER TIRES

In support of its growing array of regulatory programs concerning motor vehicle emissions and fuel economy, the federal government began paying attention to tire rolling resistance in the 1970s.[7] When J1269 was issued in 1979, EPA was one of the first organizations to use it to test new passenger tires. Having observed a large positive effect on fuel economy from the mass introduction of radial-ply tires, EPA suspected that variations in the rolling resistance of tires installed on new vehicles could have measurable effects on both emissions and fuel economy test results. The agency therefore began testing common passenger tires for rolling resistance to ascertain the magnitude of this effect.

During the 25 years since EPA tested a 54-tire sample of bias- and radial-ply passenger tires, few additional data on tire rolling resistance have become publicly available for either replacement or OE passenger tires. The publicly available data sets are reviewed below, beginning with EPA's 54-tire sample from 1982 and 1983 and continuing with more recent information from *Consumer Reports,* private research consultants, and submissions to NHTSA and U.S. Department of Transportation rule-making. Of most significance, rolling resistance measurements for more than 150 new passenger tires were made publicly available by three major tire companies during the course of this study. While the data set has limitations, it contains data on many new tires currently on the market and supplemental data on each tire's speed rating, size, traction and tread wear ratings, tread depth, and retail price.

Unless otherwise specified, all RRCs in the data sets discussed below were derived by using the J1269 procedure on new tires. For reasons given in the Appendix, the committee is confident that this test procedure leads to ordinal rankings of tires in terms of rolling resistance that are comparable with those that would be expected from applying the J2452 procedure. Because it has been used for more than 25 years, the J1269 procedure allows for comparisons of RRC measurements across data sets that span two decades or more. However, as with all testing conducted at different times, by different laboratories, and with different equipment, some of the observed variability in RRCs—both across and within data sets—may be attributable to the testing mechanisms themselves. The committee acknowledges this potential but has no reason to believe that any testing

---

[7] Schuring (1980) estimated that tire rolling resistance declined by 25 percent during the 1970s, almost entirely as a result of the mass introduction of radial-ply tires.

discrepancies would follow a particular pattern or be of a magnitude that would severely compromise general comparisons across data sets.

The RRC measurements from several of the data sets discussed in this section are presented in tables. The specific values are shown because some of the data sets are unpublished or their original sources are difficult to obtain. The RRC data supplied by the Rubber Manufacturers Association (RMA), however, are too lengthy to provide in this report. The RMA data accompany the downloadable version of this report at the TRB website location trb.org/news/blurb_detail.asp?id=5973.

## EPA Measurements, 1982–1983

EPA conducted the first government-sponsored measurements of new-tire rolling resistance during the early 1980s with the SAE J1269 test procedure (Thompson and Reineman 1981; Egeler 1984). The agency funded testing of 252 individual tires from 20 manufacturer brand names and 54 model lines. The sample consisted of 36 radial-ply and 18 bias-ply lines. The tires were sampled to be representative of the most popular tires at that time and were believed to include more than half of the tire lines in the replacement market. All of the tires tested were P195/75 with 14-inch rim diameters, which was believed to be the most common size at the time. Four to six tires were tested from each tire line to calculate an average rolling resistance for each of the 54 models.

Table 3-2 presents the results only for the 36 radial-ply lines tested by EPA. The results for the 18 bias-ply tires, which are no longer in common use, are omitted. All of the tires were tested when new, after the break-in protocols of the SAE test procedure were followed. The reported RRCs for the 36 tires ranged from 0.0098 to 0.0138, with a mean of 0.0113. In every case but one, the radial-ply tires exhibited significantly lower new-tire rolling resistance than the bias-ply lines. The average RRC for radial-ply tires was more than 20 percent lower than that of the bias-ply group.

## Michelin and Other Tire Company Data Submitted to NHTSA Rulemaking (1994–1995)

In 1994, when NHTSA proposed adding a fuel economy label for passenger tires as part of the Uniform Tire Quality Grading (UTQG)

**TABLE 3-2** EPA New-Tire Rolling Resistance Measurements for 36 Radial-Ply Passenger Tires, 1982–1983

| Replacement Tire Brand and Line | Rolling Resistance Coefficient (Measured When Tire Is New) |
|---|---|
| BF Goodrich Lifesaver XLM | 0.0098 |
| Uniroyal Steeler | 0.0100 |
| Delta Radial II | 0.0101 |
| Laramie Glass Rider | 0.0102 |
| Atlas Silveraire | 0.0104 |
| Firestone Deluxe Champion Radial | 0.0104 |
| Michelin XMW | 0.0105 |
| Multi-Mile XL | 0.0105 |
| Montgomery Ward Runabout | 0.0106 |
| General Steel Radial | 0.0106 |
| Uniroyal Tiger Paw | 0.0107 |
| JC Penney Mileagemaker Plus | 0.0108 |
| Goodyear Arriva | 0.0109 |
| Kelly Springfield Navigator | 0.0109 |
| General Dual Steel III | 0.0109 |
| Multi-Mile Supreme | 0.0110 |
| Goodyear Custom Poly-Steel | 0.0110 |
| K-Mart KM-225 | 0.0110 |
| Dayton Quadra | 0.0111 |
| Delta Durasteel | 0.0111 |
| Firestone 721 | 0.0112 |
| Dayton Blue Ribbon | 0.0115 |
| JC Penney Mileagemaker XP | 0.0115 |
| Firestone Trax 12 | 0.0117 |
| Sears Road Handler 78 | 0.0118 |
| Summit Steel | 0.0118 |
| Dunlop Goldseal | 0.0119 |
| Montgomery Ward Grappler | 0.0121 |
| Sears Weather Handler | 0.0121 |
| Goodyear Tiempo | 0.0123 |
| Cooper Lifeline Glass Belt | 0.0123 |
| Armstrong SXA | 0.0123 |
| Dunlop Generation IV | 0.0125 |
| Cooper Lifeliner Steel Belt | 0.0126 |
| Michelin XVS | 0.0136 |
| Armstrong Coronet All-Season | 0.0138 |
| Mean | 0.0113 |
| Median | 0.0113 |

NOTE: Four to six tires were tested from each line, totaling 252 tires. All tested tires were P195/75/R15 or equivalent ER-78-15. The sample was selected on the basis of tire sales popularity. In addition to the 36 radial tire lines, EPA tested 18 bias-ply tire lines. The bias-ply tires (including some bias-belt tires) had an RRC averaging 20.2 percent higher than that of the radial-ply tires.
SOURCE: Egeler 1984.

system,[8] most tire companies opposed the proposal in comments submitted to the agency (NHTSA 1995). Michelin was the only major tire company to approve of the proposed addition to the UTQG. In its initial comments to NHTSA, Michelin reported RRCs for nine OE and 37 replacement tires measured when they were new.[9] The 46 tires were from a variety of lines manufactured by Michelin, Bridgestone, Cooper, Goodyear, and other tire makers (Table 3-3). The basis for the sample was not given, nor were the tire sizes. The nine OE tires had an average RRC of 0.0091 and fell within a range from 0.0073 to 0.0105. The 37 replacement tires had an average RRC of 0.0112 and fell within a range from 0.0087 to 0.0143.

In a submission to NHTSA the following year (1995),[10] Michelin provided the rolling resistance specifications for 24 OE tires that were supplied to 10 automobile manufacturers for several Model Year 1995 vehicles. Again, the RRCs were measured when the tires were new. The values ranged from 0.0077 to 0.0114 (Table 3-3). Michelin also tested replacement tires from six tires lines, including three consisting of P215/70/R15 tires and three consisting of P235/75/R15 tires. The tires were from Michelin, Goodyear, and Continental. The RRCs for the six tire lines ranged from 0.0089 to 0.0128.

In other comments to NHTSA in the same rulemaking, Goodyear provided its own estimates of the range of RRCs commonly found among OE and replacement tires. It estimated ranges of 0.0067 to 0.0152 for new OE tires and 0.0073 to 0.0131 for new replacement tires, although it did not name the tires included.[11]

## EPA Coastdown and Fuel Economy Tests (2001)

Since its initial rolling resistance tests in the early 1980s, EPA has performed additional work on tire energy performance, mainly in support

---

[8] *Federal Register*, Vol. 60, No. 100, May 24, 1995. NHTSA Docket No. 94-30.

[9] NHTSA Docket No. 94-30. Exhibit B of letter from Clarence Hermann, Michelin, to Oron Kerr, NHTSA, dated August 9, 1994.

[10] NHTSA Docket No. 94-30. Appendix 2-1 and Appendix 2-2 in letter from Clarence Hermann, Michelin, dated August 31, 1995.

[11] See page III-12 of NHTSA Preliminary Regulatory Evaluation, NPRM Light Vehicle Uniform Tire Quality Grading Standards, Office of Regulatory Analysis, Plans, and Policy, May 1995.

**TABLE 3-3** OE and Replacement Passenger Tire RRCs Measured for Tires When New, Reported by Michelin in 1994 and 1995

| Brand | Tire Line | | RRC |
|---|---|---|---|
| **OE Tire Measurements Reported in 1994** | | | |
| Goodyear | Invicta GLR | | 0.0073 |
| Dunlop | SP23V | | 0.0077 |
| Michelin | XW4 | | 0.008 |
| Michelin | LXI | | 0.0088 |
| Firestone | FR680 | | 0.0094 |
| Michelin | XGT4 | | 0.0098 |
| Michelin | MX4 | | 0.01 |
| Firestone | Supreme | | 0.0105 |
| Firestone | FR480 | | 0.0105 |
| | | Mean | 0.0091 |
| | | Median | 0.0094 |
| **OE Tire Measurements Reported in 1995** | | | |
| Michelin | XW4 | P195/70/R14 S | 0.0077 |
| Michelin | MXV4 | P205/60/R16 H | 0.0078 |
| Uniroyal | Tiger Paw AWP | P155/60/R13 S | 0.008 |
| Michelin | XW4 | P215/70/R15 S | 0.0082 |
| Michelin | MX4 Green X | P195/65/R15 S | 0.0084 |
| Michelin | XW4 | P195/70/R14 S | 0.0084 |
| Uniroyal | Tiger Paw AWP | P215/65/R16 | 0.0087 |
| Michelin | Energy MX4 | P235/60/R15 H | 0.0088 |
| BF Goodrich | Touring T/A | P205/70/R15 S | 0.0088 |
| Uniroyal | Tiger Paw AWP | P205/75/R15 S | 0.0089 |
| Michelin | MXV4 | P205/60/R15 V | 0.009 |
| BF Goodrich | Touring T/A | P195/65/R15 S | 0.009 |
| Michelin | MXV4 | P155/60/R13 S | 0.009 |
| BF Goodrich | Touring T/A | P205/70/R15 H | 0.0091 |
| Michelin | XW4 | P215/65/R15 S | 0.0093 |
| Michelin | MXV4 | P205/65/R15 | 0.0095 |
| BF Goodrich | Touring T/A | P175/70/R14 S | 0.0097 |
| Michelin | Energy MX4 | P195/65/R15 H | 0.0098 |
| Michelin | MXV4 | P205/60/R15 H | 0.0099 |
| Michelin | XW4 | P225/60/R16 S | 0.01 |
| Michelin | MXV4 | P215/65/R16 T | 0.0103 |
| Michelin | MXV4 | P165/65/R15 | 0.0105 |
| Michelin | Energy MX4 | P185/65/R14 H | 0.0107 |
| Uniroyal | Tiger Paw AWP | P145/60/R15 T | 0.0114 |
| | | Mean | 0.0092 |
| | | Median | 0.009 |

| Brand | Tire Line | RRC |
|---|---|---|
| **Replacement Tire Measurements Reported in 1994** | | |
| Goodyear | Invicta GL | 0.0087 |
| Goodrich | Momenta S/E | 0.0095 |
| Michelin | MXL | 0.0097 |
| Cooper | Cornell 800 | 0.0098 |
| Kelly | Kelly Explorer 400 | 0.01 |
| UG | Cientra | 0.01 |
| Goodrich | Touring T/A | 0.01 |
| Uniroyal | Tiger Paw A/S | 0.01 |
| Kelly | Charger | 0.0102 |
| Kleber | CP75 | 0.0103 |
| UG | Defender SRX +4 | 0.0104 |
| Goodrich | Radial T/A | 0.0105 |
| Cooper | Trendsetter II A/W | 0.0105 |
| Uniroyal | Rally GTS | 0.0105 |
| Michelin | XGTH4 | 0.0107 |
| Goodrich | Lifesaver A/W | 0.0107 |
| Kelly | Voyager 1000 Touring | 0.0109 |
| Goodrich | The Advantage | 0.011 |
| Cooper | Lifeliner Classic | 0.011 |
| Kelly | Navigator 800S | 0.0112 |
| Uniroyal | Tiger Paw XTM | 0.0112 |
| Cooper | Monogram A/W | 0.0113 |
| UG | UG Liberator II+ | 0.0113 |
| Goodrich | Tour T/A | 0.0114 |
| Armstrong | Sears Guardsman | 0.0116 |
| Cooper | Cobra GTS | 0.0117 |
| Yokohama | Y376A | 0.0118 |
| Uniroyal | Tiger Paw | 0.012 |
| Michelin | XGTH4 | 0.0121 |
| Firestone | FTX | 0.0121 |
| Goodyear | Aquatred | 0.0122 |
| Goodyear | Eagle GA | 0.0124 |
| Firestone | FTX | 0.0127 |
| Sumitomo | HTR4 | 0.0127 |
| Michelin | MX4 | 0.0134 |
| Goodyear | Eagle GA | 0.0137 |
| Dunlop | D60A2 | 0.0143 |
| | Mean | 0.0112 |
| | Median | 0.0103 |

*(continued on next page)*

**TABLE 3-3** *(continued)* OE and Replacement Passenger Tire RRCs Measured for Tires When New, Reported by Michelin in 1994 and 1995

| Brand | Tire Line | | RRC |
|---|---|---|---|
| **Replacement Tire Measurements Reported in 1995** | | | |
| Michelin | XH4 | P215/70/R15 | 0.0089 |
| BF Goodrich | The Advantage | P215/70/R15 | 0.0097 |
| General | Grabber AP | P235/75/R15 | 0.0102 |
| Goodyear | Wrangler | P235/75/R15 | 0.0106 |
| Uniroyal | Laredo AWT | P235/75/R15 | 0.0123 |
| Goodyear | Aquatred | P215/70/R15 | 0.0127 |
| | | Mean | 0.0107 |
| | | Median | 0.0104 |

of its climate change programs. In 2001, it conducted load and fuel economy tests on several tires installed on the same vehicle (Automotive Testing Laboratories 2002). The results of this work are presented here for informational purposes only. The agency intended to use the test results to develop a tire ranking system for rolling resistance, to be made available on its website or in a "Green Car Guide."[12] Because EPA did not measure RRCs for the tires tested, the data are difficult to compare with other measurement data and are not referred to again in this report.

Five Model Year 2001 passenger vehicles (Dodge Caravan, Ford F150, Chevrolet Suburban, Toyota Camry, and Honda Civic) were tested when equipped with their original tires and with popular replacement tires. None of the OE tires was new; each set had been in service between 2,000 and 14,700 miles. Four of the vehicles were tested with one set of new replacement tires, and a fifth vehicle (Camry) was tested with five sets of new replacement tires.

Two separate tests were carried out to measure the forces associated with tires. The first test, designed to measure variations in road load, was conducted on a 7.5-mile test track. Each vehicle was driven to a speed of 125 km/h and then placed in neutral to coast. Deceleration was recorded at various intervals to calculate road load forces. Higher deduced loads were assumed to be indicative of higher rolling resistance. At the 50-mph

---

[12] The agency lacked the resources for more comprehensive tire testing to develop the guide for tires.

interval, the road load force was 4.4 to 14.3 percent higher for the replacement tires on four of the tested vehicles. In the case of the Camry, four of the five replacement tires exhibited lower road load forces than did the OE tires (and presumably lower rolling resistance), by 0.2 to 10.6 percent. No explanation of why the Camry results differed from those of the other vehicles was offered.

EPA conducted coastdown measurements for each tire group on a chassis dynamometer. The resistance forces at 50 mph showed a similar pattern; the replacement tires measured higher loads by 2 to 5.7 percent. The exception was the Camry. For that vehicle, the measured rolling resistance of four of the five replacement tires was lower than that of the OE tires by 13 to 26 percent.

EPA also tested the vehicles and their tire groupings for fuel economy by using the federal test procedure. Measurements of fuel economy were lower by 0.5 to 5.5 percent in four of the five vehicles when equipped with replacement tires. Meanwhile, measurements of vehicle fuel economy for the Camry were higher by 1.3 to 10.4 percent for four of the five replacement tires.

## Ecos Consulting Data (2002)

With funding from the Energy Foundation, Ecos Consulting—a private consulting organization—sponsored tests measuring the rolling resistance of 48 new replacement tires during 2002. The tires were selected to cover the products of several manufacturers and to include a mix of sizes and types. The rolling resistance measurements were conducted under the SAE J1269 test procedure. The 48 tires originally included seven light truck (LT-metric) and seven specialty winter tires. These 14 tires are excluded from the data set as it is examined here, given this study's focus on passenger tires. The 34 remaining passenger tires consisted of four groupings of sizes: P185/70R14, P235/75R15, P205/55R16, and P245/75R16. About one-third were from performance lines (H-rated and above). The RRC measurements are shown in Table 3-4. They range from 0.00615 to 0.01328, with an average of 0.0102 and a median of 0.0104.

Because this data set is contemporary and the tire names and sizes are identified, the committee was able to collect supplemental information for each tire, including its UTQG system grades, tread depth, and retail

**TABLE 3-4**  Rolling Resistance Coefficients for 34 Passenger Tires, Measured When New by Ecos Consulting in 2002

| Tire Manufacturer | Tire Line | Size | RRC |
|---|---|---|---|
| Bridgestone/Firestone | B381 | P185/70/R14 | 0.0062 |
| Continental | Ameri-G4S WS | P235/75/R15 | 0.0078 |
| Goodyear | Invicta GL | P235/75/R15 | 0.0081 |
| Continental | ContiTouring Contact CH95 | P205/55/R16 | 0.0083 |
| Uniroyal | Tiger Paw AWP | P185/70/R14 | 0.0088 |
| Michelin | Energy MXV4 Plus | P205/55/R16 | 0.009 |
| Goodyear | Eagle RS A | P205/55/R16 | 0.0092 |
| Bridgestone/Firestone | Long Trail T/A SL | P245/75/R16 | 0.0092 |
| Michelin | Pilot Sport Cup | P205/55/R16 | 0.0092 |
| Sumitomo | HTR 200 | P185/70/R14 | 0.0092 |
| Pirelli | P6000 | P205/55/R16 | 0.0095 |
| General | Grabber AP SL | P235/75/R15 | 0.0097 |
| Goodyear | Integrity | P185/70/R14 | 0.0097 |
| Bridgestone/Firestone | FR680 WS | P235/75/R15 | 0.0102 |
| Dunlop | SP40 A/S | P185/70/R14 | 0.0103 |
| Michelin | LTX M/S | P245/75/R16 | 0.0103 |
| Bridgestone/Firestone | Dueler A/T D693 | P245/75/R16 | 0.0103 |
| Bridgestone/Firestone | Wilderness AT | P235/75/R15 | 0.0105 |
| Kumho | Venture AT | P245/75/R16 | 0.0105 |
| Bridgestone/Firestone | Potenza RE92 | P185/70/R14 | 0.0107 |
| Michelin | Harmony | P185/70/R14 | 0.0107 |
| Goodyear | Regatta 2 | P185/70/R14 | 0.0108 |
| Michelin | Symmetry | P185/70/R14 | 0.0108 |
| Bridgestone/Firestone | Turanza LS-H | P205/55/R16 | 0.0109 |
| Bridgestone/Firestone | Turanza LS-T | P185/70/R14 | 0.0109 |
| Bridgestone/Firestone | Affinity Touring | P235/75/R15 | 0.011 |
| Michelin | Pilot Sport | P205/55/R16 | 0.0111 |
| Goodyear | Eagle F1 GS-D3 | P205/55/R16 | 0.0112 |
| Dunlop | SP Sport A2 SL | P205/55/R16 | 0.0113 |
| Goodyear | Aquatred 3 | P185/70/R14 | 0.0113 |
| Goodyear | Conquest AT | P245/75/R16 | 0.0114 |
| Bridgestone/Firestone | Firehawk SZ50EP | P205/55/R16 | 0.012 |
| Goodyear | Eagle GT II | P205/55/R16 | 0.0121 |
| Michelin | Pilot Sport A/S | P205/55/R16 | 0.0133 |
| | | Mean | 0.0102 |
| | | Median | 0.0104 |

SOURCE: Ecos Consulting, personal communication, August 2005.

prices. The data are analyzed later in the report, along with tire data from other sources.

## Consumers Union Tests (2003–2004)

Consumers Union periodically tests categories of passenger tires for various performance attributes of interest to consumers and publishes the results in *Consumer Reports*. In recent years, it has tested passenger tires commonly used on SUVs and pickup trucks (November 2004) and performance tires used mainly on passenger cars (speed rated H and above) (November 2003). A total of 40 tires were tested, including 22 all-season SUV/pickup tires and 18 performance-rated tires. The 22 SUV/pickup tires were all size P235/70/R16 with speed ratings of S or T. The sizes of the 18 performance tires were not given.

Presumably, rolling resistance was measured when the tires were new, although *Consumer Reports* did not report the rolling resistance values derived from the tests or the exact test procedures used—except to note that measurements were taken on a dynamometer at 65 mph. The results were presented in a qualitative manner in *Consumer Reports*. Of the 40 tires tested, the rolling resistance of 21 was characterized as excellent or very good, 15 as good or fair, and 4 as poor. *Consumer Reports* stated that the difference in vehicle fuel economy (miles per gallon) between a tire rated as excellent and one rated as poor is about 2 percent at 65 mph. Results from multiple sizes within a tire line were not given.

The *Consumer Reports* results are not examined further in this study because of the qualitative nature of the ratings information. Some of the tires tested by Consumers Union (including the exact sizes) also appear in the RMA data set discussed later. From this limited comparison of the two data sets, it appears that *Consumer Reports* characterizes tires with RRCs below 0.01 as excellent, between 0.01 and 0.011 as very good or good, and above 0.011 as poor.

## OEM Interviews (2005)

Interested in learning more about the rolling resistance characteristics of OE tires, committee members and staff interviewed representatives from several OEMs: General Motors, Daimler Chrysler, and Ford Motor

Company. The interviews yielded information on rolling resistance values and ranges for new OE tires, as well as projected effects of incremental changes in tire rolling resistance on motor vehicle fuel economy. The meetings also provided insights into OEM expectations about future trends in rolling resistance and the relationship between rolling resistance and other tire performance characteristics, which are discussed later in this report. Because the discussions with the OEMs involved proprietary information, the committee agreed not to disclose the identity of individual companies giving specific information.

As has been noted, all automobile manufacturers maintain staff with tire expertise and have tire testing capabilities. Rolling resistance is an important consideration in specifying tires for most vehicle models, but specifications differ by vehicle and by tire depending on the other performance capabilities of interest for the vehicle class and type. As a preface to their comments, all three OEMs emphasized that the resulting balance of performance attributes changes over time as tire technologies improve. All have observed progressive improvements in tire properties over time; consequently, comparisons of tires at different technology levels may not reveal the same pattern of trade-offs required to achieve a specific balance of capabilities and tire supply costs.

When asked to approximate the range of rolling resistance values specified for their new tires, the OEMs noted that their individual ranges may differ in part because of variability in tire testing equipment, applied correction factors, and the reference conditions used in calculating and reporting specific RRCs. They cautioned that this variability alone could result in RRC differentials of as much as ±20 percent among the ranges reported by each company and in comparison with RRCs observed among replacement tires. All of the OEMs reported measuring and specifying rolling resistance under the SAE J2452 test procedure because the results can be fitted into models for the federal driving cycles used in emissions and fuel economy testing. Achieving federal emissions and fuel economy targets is a major reason why OEMs are concerned with rolling resistance.

One of the OEMs indicated that the following new-tire rolling resistance values are typical for four general categories of OE passenger tires:

- All-season, 0.007;
- Touring, 0.008;

- Performance, 0.01; and
- Light truck passenger, 0.0075 to 0.0095.

The all-season and touring tires are the most common tires installed on its passenger cars, with the latter more common for more expensive and higher trim level cars.

Another OEM provided the following new-tire rolling resistance ranges for similar tire categories, which were derived by using the SAE J2452 test procedure and reported by using the Standard Mean Equivalent Rolling Force conditions described in the Appendix:

- All-season, 0.005 to 0.0062;
- Touring, 0.0058 to 0.0075;
- Performance, 0.0065 to 0.0083; and
- High performance, 0.009.

The company did not provide typical rolling resistance values for light truck passenger tires.

The final OEM did not provide rolling resistance ranges but offered relevant observations with regard to its experience in testing and specifying rolling resistance. It has observed significant changes in the rolling resistance characteristics of a tire during break-in and initial operation. The company has found that tread rubber changes permanently during the first 4,000 miles of use, resulting in lower rolling resistance. Thus, in general, the company relies on vehicle coastdown testing for rolling resistance in evaluating tires for application on its vehicles (similar to the test methods used by EPA in 2001 described above). The company has found this test method to be more reliable for selecting tires that can help achieve vehicle emissions and fuel economy targets, since changes in rolling resistance occur during tire break-in.

In commenting on future tire developments, the OEMs observed that current tire trends are already having mixed effects on rolling resistance. The trends toward larger rim diameters and lower aspect ratios among performance tires are generally helpful in reducing rolling resistance, but they are normally accompanied by the addition of hysteretic material to improve cornering and stopping capabilities, which the OEMs believe may be increasing rolling resistance. Run-flat tires, which are becoming more popular, appear to have at least 20 percent higher rolling resistance than the conventional OE tires supplied on the same vehicle, in part because run-flat tires have additional structural material and mass. However, one model of run-flat tire was reported to have lower rolling resistance because of its internal bracing, which reduces deformation.

One OEM reported that tires installed on hybrid vehicles are generally not specified any differently from those installed on nonhybrid cars designed to achieve high fuel economy. Another noted that the attention given to tire rolling resistance can be expected to increase with the advent of hybrid drivetrains and technologies such as cylinder cutout, since the fuel economy effects are greater. In some cases, low-rolling-resistance tires have enabled increases in the operating range of cylinder cutout.

## RMA Data Set (2005)

Through RMA, three major tire manufacturers—Michelin, Goodyear, and Bridgestone—provided the committee with rolling resistance measurements, UTQG system grades, and speed ratings for 162 passenger tires of varying sizes and affiliated brands (e.g., Uniroyal, Firestone, BFGoodrich). The Michelin portion of the data set consisted of 135 tires from more than three dozen lines in the replacement market. Bridgestone provided data for 24 tires from five lines, including five OE tires. Goodyear data covered 13 tires from four lines, including three OE tires. Originally included among the Michelin data were 44 light truck and winter tires, which the committee excluded from the main data set.

In all cases, the RRC measurements were obtained with the SAE J1269 test procedure. All of the RRCs were derived from measurements of tires tested when new. In providing the data, the three tire companies emphasized that the RRC values reported by each company could exhibit variability in part because of the differences in testing equipment used for RRC measurement. Such testing variability, coupled with the variability in the number and selection of tires reported by each company, precludes comparisons of patterns across tire companies. Hence, the data reported by the three tire companies are examined in the aggregate and are referred to in the following as the RMA data set.

The RMA data set includes tires of many sizes and speed ratings. Table 3-5 contains summary statistics for the data set derived from three

**TABLE 3-5**  Summary Statistics, 2005 RMA
Passenger Tire Data Set

| Item | Number | Percent |
|---|---|---|
| Manufacturer | | |
| Bridgestone | 24 | 14.8 |
| Michelin | 125 | 77.2 |
| Goodyear | 13 | 8.0 |
| Tire brands/lines | | |
| Bridgestone | 5 | |
| Michelin | >30 | |
| Goodyear | 4 | |
| Speed rating | | |
| S, T | 97 | 59.9 |
| H, V | 31 | 19.1 |
| W, Y, Z | 34 | 21.0 |
| Rim size (in.) | | |
| 13 | 5 | 3.1 |
| 14 | 18 | 11.1 |
| 15 | 47 | 29.0 |
| 16 | 43 | 26.5 |
| 17 | 30 | 18.5 |
| 18 | 10 | 6.2 |
| 19+ | 9 | 5.6 |
| Tread depth (where known)[a] (in.) | | |
| 9/32 | 7 | 5.1 |
| 10/32 | 58 | 42.0 |
| 10.5/32 | 6 | 4.3 |
| 11/32 | 40 | 29.0 |
| 11.5/32 | 2 | 1.4 |
| 12/32 | 8 | 5.8 |
| 13/32 or more | 17 | 12.3 |
| Tire weight (where known)[b] (lb) | | |
| <20 | 21 | 13.6 |
| 20–22 | 31 | 20.1 |
| 23–25 | 32 | 20.8 |
| 26–30 | 28 | 18.2 |
| 31–35 | 23 | 14.9 |
| 36+ | 23 | 14.9 |

NOTE: Replacement tires in sample = 154; OE tires in sample = 8; total tires = 162.
[a] Average depth = 10.76/32 in.
[b] Average weight = 26.6 lb.

tire manufacturers. Of the 162 tires sampled, 97 (60 percent) are speed rated S or T, 31 (19 percent) are rated for performance (speed rated H or V), and 34 (21 percent) are rated for high performance (speed rated W, Y, or Z). A large majority of the tires (74 percent) have rim diameters of 15, 16, or 17 inches. In addition, three-quarters of the sampled tires have aspect ratios of 60 to 75, while the remaining tires have lower ratios (mostly 45, 50, and 55). Tire section widths range from 175 to 335 millimeters; tires with section widths between 195 and 245 millimeters account for 70 percent of the tires sampled. Among the 162 tires, there are more than 70 distinct size (section width, aspect ratio, and rim diameter) and speed rating (S, T; H, V; W, Y, Z) combinations.

It is difficult to ascertain how representative the 162 tires are of the general population of passenger tires sold each year in the United States. Data on industry shipments suggest that the above data set contains a higher-than-average percentage of performance tires. The RMA *Factbook* for 2005 indicates that tires with speed rating S or T accounted for 73 percent of replacement tire shipments in 2004, while tires with higher speed ratings—H or V and W, Y, or Z—accounted for 22 and 4 percent, respectively (RMA 2005, 22).

In addition, the RMA data were provided without information on the sampling methodology. Some of the data points represent single tests on individual tires, and other data represent more than one test. While these shortcomings limit the degree to which definitive findings can be attributed to analyses of the data, the RMA data set is by far the largest single source of publicly available data on rolling resistance for new tires sold in the United States. In this respect, it offers many opportunities for analyzing rolling resistance levels and relationships with respect to other attributes such as wear resistance, traction, size, selling price, and speed ratings. To expand these analytic opportunities, the committee supplemented the information provided by the tire companies with publicly available data on each tire's tread depth, weight, and retail prices obtained from manufacturer and tire retailer websites. These data are analyzed in Chapters 4 and 5 to assess possible relationships with rolling resistance.

The focus of the remainder of this chapter is on the new-tire rolling resistance values observed in the RMA data. Because the data set contains

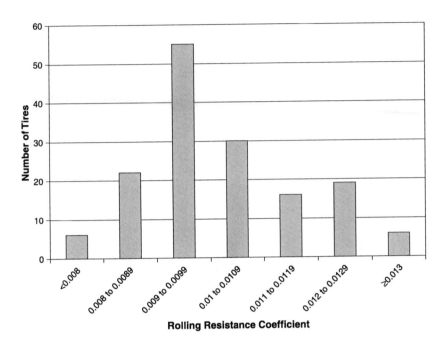

**FIGURE 3-2** Distribution of tires in the RMA data set by RRC.

only eight tires identified as current OE tires, which is too few for useful comparisons, the emphasis of the statistical assessment is on the 154 replacement tires in the data set.[13]

*General Variability in Rolling Resistance*

The range of RRCs observed for the 154 replacement tires in the RMA data set is 0.0065 to 0.0133, with a mean and median of 0.0102 and 0.0099, respectively (Figure 3-2). More than half (55 percent) of the tires have an RRC between 0.009 and 0.011. Coefficients below 0.008 or above 0.013 can be characterized as unusually low or high, and such values occur in less than 8 percent of the tires sampled.

---

[13] The committee cannot know how many of the replacement tires in the data set were originally developed for the OE market or are still being used for some OE applications.

### Rolling Resistance Variability by Tire Size and Speed Rating

A simple sorting of the data by speed rating reveals that the performance-rated tires have a slightly higher-than-average rolling resistance. The average for S and T tires is 0.0098, while the averages for H, V and W, Y, Z tires are 0.0101 and 0.0113, respectively. This pattern suggests a relationship between RRC and speed rating. However, performance tires are more likely to have lower aspect ratios, wider section widths, and larger rim diameters than tires with lower speed ratings. Thus, geometric differences in tires may contribute to rolling resistance differentials just as much as the design elements intended to augment performance.

A sorting of the data by rim diameter suggests that tire dimensions can indeed have an effect on rolling resistance measurements. Tires with a rim diameter of 15 inches or lower have an average rolling resistance of 0.0106, more than 10 percent above the average of 0.0093 for the tires with a higher rim diameter.

### Rolling Resistance Variability Among Comparable Tires

Multivariate statistical analyses are required to control for the many tire design variables that may be related to rolling resistance. Such an analysis is performed in the next chapter to shed light on the full array of relationships between rolling resistance and other tire characteristics such as tread depth and tread wear. Nevertheless, a simple descriptive sorting of the data by tire speed ratings and size dimensions offers some insights into the variations in RRC that occur within groupings of tires having the same size and speed ratings. Figure 3-3 shows the distribution of RRCs for the seven most popular speed rating–size configurations in the RMA data set, which includes 51 of the 154 replacement tires in the data set. The sorting reveals wide ranges in RRCs within such groupings of like tires. In all seven groupings, the difference between the highest and lowest value is at least 18 percent, and most of the differentials exceed 25 percent.

### Assessment of Rolling Resistance Data

Table 3-6 summarizes the RRCs from the above-referenced data sets, starting with the early EPA data and ending with the RMA data from 2005. As noted, the 1982–1983 EPA measurements confirmed the large reductions in rolling resistance caused by the introduction of radial-ply tires, although

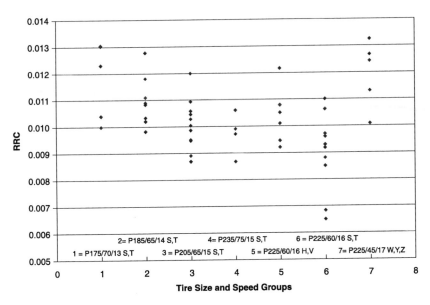

**FIGURE 3-3** Distribution of RRCs for tires in the most common size and speed rating groupings, RMA data set.

most RRCs for radial tires in 1982–1983 exceeded 0.01. The Michelin-reported data for replacement tires on the market in the mid-1990s show further progress in reducing rolling resistance, especially in the number of tires achieving RRCs below 0.01. The most recent data, from Ecos Consulting in 2002 and RMA in 2005, reveal additional reductions in the average and median rolling resistance. Nearly 20 percent of the tires sampled in these more recent (2002 and 2005) data sets had rolling resistance measurements of 0.009 or less. In comparison, none of the tires sampled by EPA in the early 1980s, and only two tires in the Michelin-reported data from 1994 and 1995, had an RRC lower than 0.009.

Most notable are the gains made among the top-performing tires with respect to rolling resistance. The 25 percent (or quartile) of tires having the lowest RRCs in the 1982–1983 data set had an average RRC of 0.0103. This compares with an average RRC of 0.0085 for the same quartile for the combined 2002 and 2005 data. Figure 3-4 shows a plot of the RRCs from the various data sets. It displays the persistence of tires at the high

**TABLE 3-6** Summary of Data Sets Containing Rolling Resistance Measurements for OE and Replacement Passenger Tires, 1982 to 2005

| Data Set | Tire Lines | Tire Sizes | RRC Range | RRC Average |
|---|---|---|---|---|
| **Replacement Tires** | | | | |
| EPA 1982–1983 | 36 from several tire makers | 195/75/R15 | 0.00979 to 0.01381 | 0.01131 |
| Michelin 1994 | 37 from several tire makers | Not given | 0.0087 to 0.01430 | 0.01117 |
| Goodyear 1994 | Not given | Not given | 0.0073 to 0.0131 | Not given |
| Michelin 1995 | 6 from three tire makers | 215/70/R15, 235/75/R15 | 0.0997 to 0.0102 | 0.0108 |
| Ecos Consulting 2002 | 34 from several tire makers | 185/70/R14 | 0.0062 to 0.0133 | 0.0102 |
| | | 205/55/R16 | | |
| | | 235/75/R15 | | |
| | | 245/75/R16 | | |
| RMA 2005 | 154 from three tire makers, mostly Michelin brands | Various | 0.0065 to 0.0133 | 0.0102 |
| **OE Tires** | | | | |
| Michelin 1994 | 9 from several tire makers | Not given | 0.0073 to 0.0105 | 0.0091 |
| Goodyear 1994 | Not given | Not given | 0.0067 to 0.0152 | Not given |
| Michelin 1995 | 24 from Michelin brands | Various | 0.0077 to 0.0114 | 0.0092 |
| OEM interviews 2005 | Multiple tire lines | | | |
| | All-season | | 0.005 to 0.007 | |
| | Touring | | 0.0058 to 0.008 | |
| | Performance | | 0.0065 to 0.01 | |
| | Light truck (passenger tires) | | 0.0075 to 0.0095 | |
| RMA 2005 | 8 from Bridgestone and Goodyear brands | Various | 0.007 to 0.0095 | 0.00838 |

NOTE: All of the rolling resistance values in the table were derived by using the SAE J1269 test procedure with the exception of the ranges given by automobile manufacturers for current OE tires. These values are estimates by OEMs on the basis of the SAE J2452 test procedure. See the Appendix for an explanation and comparison of the two SAE rolling resistance test procedures.

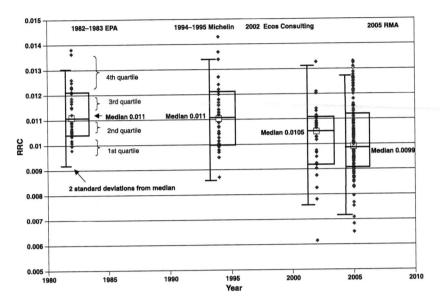

**FIGURE 3-4** Rolling resistance values for passenger tire samples, 1982 to 2005.

end of the RRC spectrum in all data sets, across all periods. In 1982–1983, the quartile of tires with the highest RRCs had an average coefficient of 0.0126. In the combined data for 2002 and 2005, this quartile had comparable RRCs, averaging 0.0125.

A possible explanation for the widening spread in RRCs among today's tires is the proliferation of tire sizes and speed ratings. The 1982–1983 EPA data are for a single tire size (P195/75/15). In that period, speed ratings were uncommon in North America. Today's replacement tires—as represented in the 2002 and 2005 data sets—include many high-performance tires. These tires, with speed ratings of W, Y, and Z, account for a disproportionate share of tires with high RRCs, as shown in Figure 3-5. Indeed, they account for most tires having RRCs greater than 0.012, whereas S and T tires (which are not considered performance tires) account for all of the values observed below 0.008. Nevertheless, Figure 3-5 also shows a persistent spread in RRCs, even when rim diameter and speed ratings are controlled for. Speed rating is not the only factor affecting rolling resistance. About one-third of the high-performance tires have RRCs below 0.01, and about 20 percent of the S and T tires have RRCs greater than 0.011.

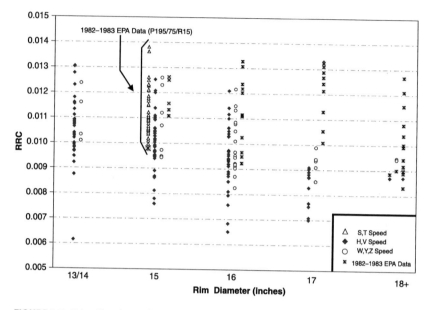

**FIGURE 3-5** Distribution of rolling resistance coefficients in 2002 and 2005 data sets compared with distribution in 1982–1983 EPA data set, controlling for rim size and speed rating.

There is an evident relationship between rim diameter and rolling resistance that warrants closer examination when the combined 2002 and 2005 data are compared with the 1982–1983 EPA data. Many of the S and T tires that have higher RRCs in the 2002 and 2005 data possess rim diameters of 13 and 14 inches. EPA only tested tires with 15-inch rim diameters. Among contemporary tires with 15-inch rim sizes, there are noticeably more with low RRCs than in the EPA data from two decades earlier. The entire distribution appears to have shifted downward by about 10 percent (Figure 3-5). Most of the higher RRCs continue to be found among the tires with smaller 13- and 14-inch rim sizes, nearly all of which are S and T tires.

The average retail price for the 13- and 14-inch S and T tires is about 50 percent ($60) below the average ($117) for all of the tires represented in the data for 2002 and 2005.[14] Hence, it is reasonable to ask whether the RRC distributions observed in this chapter are related in part to unex-

---

[14] Tire price information for the 2002 and 2005 data sets is presented in Chapters 4 and 5.

amined factors such as tire construction cost and life expectancy, which may have a strong correlation with other examined variables such as tire size and speed rating. More consideration is given in the following chapters to these and other aspects of tire performance that may have a bearing on rolling resistance.

## SUMMARY

Most of the energy contained in a tank of motor fuel is dissipated as unrecoverable heat from engine combustion and friction in the driveline. Some of the energy output from the engine powers vehicle accessories. Only about 12 to 20 percent of the energy originating in the fuel tank is ultimately transmitted through the vehicle's driveline as mechanical energy to turn the wheels. Rolling resistance consumes about one-third of this energy output. Aerodynamic drag and braking consume the remainder. Rolling resistance, therefore, directly consumes a small portion (one-third of the 12 to 20 percent) of the total energy expended by the vehicle.

However, reducing rolling resistance, and thus mechanical energy demand, by a given amount translates into a larger reduction in total fuel consumption because less fuel needs to be sent to the engine. The effect on total fuel consumption will depend on a number of factors, including the efficiency of the engine and driveline as well as the amount of energy used to power accessories. For most passenger vehicles, a 10 percent reduction in average rolling resistance over a period of time will lead to a 1 to 2 percent reduction in fuel consumption during that time.

The main source of rolling resistance is hysteresis, which is caused by the viscoelastic response of the rubber compounds in the tire as it rotates under load. The repeated tire deformation and recovery causes mechanical energy to be converted to heat; hence additional mechanical energy must be supplied to drive the axle. The design characteristics of a tire that affect this energy loss are its construction; geometric dimensions; and materials types, formulations, and volume. The tread, in particular, has a major role in hysteresis because it contains large amounts of viscoelastic rubber material. As tread wears, a tire's rolling resistance declines, primarily because of the reduction in the amount of viscoelastic material.

Travel speed within the range of normal city and highway driving has relatively little effect on rolling resistance. The main operating conditions that affect tire hysteresis are load, inflation pressure, alignment, and temperature. The more a tire is loaded at a given pressure, the more it deforms and suffers hysteretic losses. A tire deforms more when it is underinflated. For tires inflated to pressures of 24 to 36 psi, each 1-psi drop in inflation pressure increases the tire's rolling resistance by about 1.4 percent. This effect is greater for inflation pressures below 24 psi. Consequently, maintenance of tire pressure is important for a tire's energy performance as well as for tire wear and operating performance.

Rolling resistance is proportional to wheel load and can therefore be measured and expressed in terms of a constant RRC. Thus, tires with low RRCs have low rolling resistance. Standard test procedures have been developed to measure RRC. The vast majority of replacement passenger tires have RRCs within the range of 0.007 to 0.014 when measured new, while the range for new OE tires tends to be lower—on the order of 0.006 to 0.01. Federal fuel economy standards have prompted automobile manufacturers to demand OE tires with lower rolling resistance. Information on precisely how these lower-rolling-resistance characteristics have been achieved is proprietary.

In general, each incremental change in RRC of 0.001 will change vehicle fuel consumption by 1 to 2 percent. Thus, for an average passenger tire having a coefficient of 0.01, a 10 percent change in RRC will change vehicle fuel consumption by 1 to 2 percent. The lower end of the range is more relevant for tires having lower RRCs and operated at lower average speeds, while the higher end of the range is more relevant for tires having higher RRCs and operated at highway speeds.

Today's passenger tires offer better performance and capability than did previous generations of tires because of continued innovations and refinements in tire design, materials, and manufacturing. Significant progress has been made in reducing rolling resistance—as measured in new passenger tires—over the past 25 years. More tire models today, when measured new, have RRCs below 0.009, and the most energy-efficient tires have coefficients that are 20 to 30 percent lower than the most energy-efficient radial models of 25 years ago. Tires at the higher end of the RRC range, however, have not exhibited the same improvement, which has resulted in a widening spread in RRCs over time. The expansion of the number of tire sizes and speed categories, as well as new tire designs to meet changing vehicle and service applications (e.g., deep-grooved tread for light truck functional requirements and appearance), has likely contributed to the spread in RRCs. However, even among tires of similar size and speed rating, the difference between the tires with the highest and lowest RRCs often exceeds 20 percent.

Tires with high speed ratings (W, Y, and Z) and tires with smaller (13- and 14-inch) rim diameters account for a large share of tires with high rolling resistance. Whether such patterns are related to differences in other tire characteristics, such as size, traction, and wear resistance, is examined in the next chapter.

## REFERENCES

### Abbreviations

NHTSA    National Highway Traffic Safety Administration
NRC      National Research Council
RMA      Rubber Manufacturers Association
TRB      Transportation Research Board

Automotive Testing Laboratories. 2002. *Coastdown and Fuel Economy for Specific Vehicles and Tires.* Contract 68-C-00-126. U.S. Environmental Protection Agency, Dec.

Chang, L. Y., and J. S. Shackelton. 1983. An Overview of Rolling Resistance. *Elastometrics,* March, pp. 18–26.

Clark, S. K. 1983. A Brief History of Tire Rolling Resistance. In *Tire Rolling Resistance,* Rubber Division Symposia, Vol. 1 (D. J. Schuring, ed.), American Chemical Society, Akron, Ohio.

Clark, S. K., and R. N. Dodge. 1978. *A Handbook for the Rolling Resistance of Pneumatic Tires.* Report DOT TSC-78-1. U.S. Department of Transportation, June.

DeRaad, L. W. 1978. The Influence of Road Surface Texture on Tire Rolling Resistance. SAE Paper 780257. Presented at SAE Congress and Exposition, Detroit, Mich., Feb. 27–March 3.

Egeler, N. 1984. *Characterization of the Rolling Resistance of Aftermarket Passenger Car Tires.* Report EPA-AA-SDSB-84-5. Office of Mobile Sources, Standards Development and Support Branch, U.S. Environmental Protection Agency, Ann Arbor, Mich.

Hall, D. E., and J. C. Moreland. 2001. Fundamentals of Rolling Resistance. *Rubber Chemistry and Technology,* Vol. 74, pp. 525–539.

LaClair, T. J. 2005. Rolling Resistance. In *The Pneumatic Tire* (J. D. Walter and A. N. Gent, eds.), National Highway Traffic Safety Administration, Washington, D.C., pp. 475–532.

Mars, W. V., and J. R. Luchini. 1999. An Analytical Model for the Transient Rolling Resistance Behavior of Tires. *Tire Science and Technology*, Vol. 27, No. 3, July–Sept., pp. 161–175.

Martini, M. E. 1983. Passenger Tire Rolling Loss: A Tread Compounding Approach and Its Tradeoffs. In *Tire Rolling Resistance* (D. J. Schuring, ed.), American Chemical Society, Akron, Ohio, pp. 181–197.

NHTSA. 1995. *Light Vehicle Uniform Tire Quality Grading Standards: Notice of Proposed Rulemaking Preliminary Regulatory Evaluation.* Office of Regulatory Analysis Plans and Policy, May.

NRC. 1992. *Automotive Fuel Economy: How Far Should We Go?* National Academy Press, Washington, D.C.

NRC. 2002. *Effectiveness and Impact of Corporate Average Fuel Economy (CAFE) Standards.* National Academy Press, Washington, D.C.

Pillai, P. S., and G. S. Fielding-Russell. 1991. Effect of Aspect Ratio on Tire Rolling Resistance. *Rubber Chemistry and Technology*, Vol. 64, No. 3, pp. 641–647.

RMA. 2005. *Factbook 2005: U.S. Tire Shipment Activity Report for Statistical Year 2004.* Washington, D.C.

Ross, M. 1997. Fuel Efficiency and the Physics of Automobiles. *Contemporary Physics*, Vol. 38, No. 6, pp. 381–394.

Schuring, D. J. 1980. The Rolling Loss of Pneumatic Tires. *Rubber Chemistry and Technology*, Vol. 53, No. 3, pp. 600–727.

Schuring, D. J. 1994. Effects of Tire Rolling Loss on Vehicle Fuel Consumption. *Tire Science and Technology*, Vol. 22, No. 3, pp. 149–161.

Schuring, D. J., and S. Futamura. 1990. Rolling Loss of Pneumatic Highway Tires in the Eighties. *Rubber Chemistry and Technology*, Vol. 62, No. 3, pp. 315–367.

Small, K., and K. Van Dender. 2005. *Fuel Efficiency and Motor Vehicle Travel: The Declining Rebound Effect.* Economic Working Paper 05-06-03 (revised December).

Sovran, G., and D. Blaser. 2003. A Contribution to Understanding Automotive Fuel Economy and Its Limits. SAE Paper 2003-01-2070.

Thompson, G. D., and M. E. Reineman. 1981. Tire Rolling Resistance and Fuel Consumption. SAE Paper 810168. Presented at International Congress and Exposition, Detroit, Mich., Feb. 23–27.

TRB. 1997. *Special Report 251: Toward a Sustainable Future: Addressing the Long-Term Effects of Motor Vehicle Transportation on Climate and Ecology.* National Research Council, Washington, D.C.

Velinsky, S. A., and R. A. White. 1979. Increased Vehicle Energy Dissipation due to Changes in Road Roughness with Emphasis on Rolling Loss. SAE Paper 790653.

# 4

# Rolling Resistance, Traction, and Wear Performance of Passenger Tires

Tires have two basic operating functions in addition to carrying the weight of the vehicle: they mitigate shocks from the road surface and provide the longitudinal and lateral control forces for vehicle acceleration, steering, and braking.[1] All tires perform these functions, but not equally well. Some provide more friction for traction on dry surfaces, while others offer more traction in rain, snow, and mud. Some provide lower spring rates and more damping for shock mitigation, while others are stiffer for tighter cornering and general maneuverability. Of course, many other attributes are demanded of tires. As discussed in Chapter 3, good fuel economy performance is one. Others include low noise, slow wear, and durability and structural integrity at high speeds. Styling is especially important for some tire lines. Some of these attributes have little bearing on a tire's operating functions, but they are often key design considerations. Like other consumer products, tires are engineered in various ways to meet an assortment of operating requirements and user expectations and preferences.

Chapter 3 examined the effects of tire design, construction, and operational influences on rolling resistance, which was then related to vehicle fuel consumption. A complex picture of the numerous factors affecting tire rolling resistance and fuel economy emerged. Among the factors are tire geometry, tread compounds, inflation pressure, alignment, operating temperature, load, and tire construction type. Moreover, a change in any one of these variables was found to affect other variables, which leads to a chain of effects on rolling resistance and other tire characteristics. The

---

[1] See Walter (2005), Pottinger (2005), and French (1989) for detailed discussions of the tire's basic functions related to vehicle control.

statement of task for this study calls for an examination of these many relationships.

The statement of task also calls for the study to address factors that can affect vehicle safety and scrap tire generation. There is a public interest in tire safety and scrap tire generation, as there is in fuel economy. Some 40,000 motorists die in highway crashes each year, most in passenger cars and light trucks. Thousands more are critically injured. Improving the safety performance of the nation's highways is a public safety goal. During the past two decades, concerns about the environmental effects of tires, particularly the disposal of scrap tires, have also emerged. While aggressive recycling programs have reduced the entry of tires into the waste stream, the large number of tires discarded each year poses a continuing mitigation challenge.

The rolling resistance, traction, and wear characteristics of tires are not independent of one another, if for no other reason than their association with the tire's tread. As explained earlier, the tread has a major influence on rolling resistance because it contains much of the viscoelastic rubber in the tire that causes hysteretic energy loss. The same tread deformation contributes to the tire's traction capabilities. A loss in traction capability because of tread wear is the main reason for tire replacement. When the tread wears and traction capabilities are diminished beyond a point deemed acceptable for safe operation, especially in wet and snow conditions, the tire is normally scrapped—and thus becomes a candidate for the waste stream.

Years of tire testing and experimentation have helped tire manufacturers understand the chemical and physical relationships that affect tire traction, wear resistance, and rolling resistance. This has led to a growing appreciation—but still limited understanding—of how such factors relate to the practical outcomes of vehicle fuel consumption, crash incidence, and tire service life. Data sets examined in Chapter 3 show how rolling resistance can differ significantly from tire to tire and how these differences can translate into differentials in vehicle fuel consumption. The same data sets can be examined to gain a better understanding of the relationships among rolling resistance and other tire performance characteristics, including traction and wear resistance. The results of several statistical analyses of the available data sets are therefore presented in this chapter to explain these relationships.

Consideration is first given to traction effects, including implications for vehicle safety. Tread wear factors and their implications for scrap tires are then considered. In both cases, the paucity of public data limits the analyses and a broad extrapolation of the results. Whereas the rolling resistance coefficient (RRC) is a standard metric for characterizing and comparing tire energy performance, less comprehensive data exist in the public domain for accurate characterizations of tire traction and wear resistance. The federal Uniform Tire Quality Grading (UTQG) system ratings for traction and tread wear are the only metrics for which consistent data are widely available for a range of tires. These metrics are less precise than measures of RRC and provide only a partial indication of the underlying characteristics they seek to describe. Nevertheless, in combination with data on other tire properties, such as tread depth, their analysis can be helpful in identifying potential relationships and highlighting factors warranting further examination.

## EFFECTS ON TRACTION AND SAFETY PERFORMANCE

Most data on the involvement of tires in motor vehicle crashes cover tire structural failures, as opposed to the safety role of specific tire operating characteristics such as traction. Analyses of federal motor vehicle crash data indicate that tire problems such as flats, ruptures, and component separations contribute to about 24,000 tow-away crashes per year, or about 0.5 percent of all such crashes (NHTSA 2005, IV-7–IV-8; Gardner and Queiser 2005). The National Highway Traffic Safety Administration (NHTSA) estimates that these crashes result in 400 to 650 fatalities and about 10,000 nonfatal injuries in total. Thus the number of fatalities attributable to crashes caused by damaged tires is small, especially in comparison with the 40,000 deaths in motor crashes each year.[2] Service failures, however, do not necessarily indicate that a tire is inherently defective or unsafe (Gardner and Queiser 2005). Poor tire and wheel maintenance, such as low inflation pressure, improper mounting, and misalignment, can also precipitate failures in any tire.

---

[2] Not included in tire-related crash data is the indirect role of flat tires in causing disabled vehicles on the roadside that are subsequently struck by other vehicles.

The focus of federal safety regulations is on preventing tire structural failures that can cause the driver to lose control of the vehicle. As described in Chapter 2, the regulations prescribe a series of tests ensuring minimum tire strength, resistance to high-speed overheating, endurance, and—starting in 2007—low-pressure performance. All passenger tires must meet these minima. In practice, most tires on the market, if not all, will surpass them and offer safety margins in excess of those sought by federal regulation. In considering the safety of tires with low rolling resistance, a natural question is whether vehicles equipped with them exhibit disproportionate crash involvement because of tire structural failures. There is no apparent reason to suspect such an association, but in any case, national crash data cannot provide an answer because the rolling resistance of a tire at a crash scene cannot be determined.

More germane to this study is whether reducing tire rolling resistance will lead to changes in tire properties that are related to vehicle handling and control and thus could affect crash incidence and severity. A vehicle's tires are its only points of contact with the road. They generate all the forces that control its motion and direction, and a tire's properties clearly could be a factor in motor vehicle crashes and their avoidance. However, at what point a change in tire traction characteristics will lead to measurable changes in crash incidence and severity is unknown.

Through its National Accident Sampling System Crashworthiness Data System (NASS/CDS), NHTSA conducts detailed investigations of approximately 4,000 light vehicle crashes per year. The sample consists of police-reported crashes, which are examined for the purpose of national extrapolation. NHTSA investigators study the vehicles involved in the crash 1 to 60 days after the event. Recently, NHTSA added several tire-related elements to NASS/CDS. For vehicles involved in the sampled crashes, the investigators record the vehicle manufacturer's recommended tire size, construction, and inflation pressure. They also record the make, model, size, and type of tires used on the vehicle (although U.S. Department of Transportation tire identification numbers are not recorded); measure and record the depth of the tires' treads and inflation pressures; and record whether one or more of the tires exhibited damage and the type of damage (i.e., sidewall puncture, tread separation). Data for 2002 and 2003, which are the first full years to contain the tire details, will be released in 2006. The coverage and quality of the tire-related data have yet to be examined. The time lapse between the crash event and follow-up investigation may limit the usefulness of some of the data elements such as recorded tire pressure.

With the NASS/CDS infrastructure, NHTSA is also undertaking a national survey of passenger vehicle crashes in which investigators are mobilized to the scene of a sampled crash to obtain more timely information on the event and factors involved. The data gathered in this project, known as the National Motor Vehicle Crash Causation Survey, are intended to help identify opportunities to improve crash avoidance systems and technologies. For each vehicle involved in the crash, investigators record the Department of Transportation serial numbers on the tires if they are visible. Tire inflation pressure, tread depth, and visible evidence of damage are also recorded. Results from the first 3,000 to 4,000 crashes surveyed will be released in 2006.

As the tire-related information from these NHTSA data sets becomes available in sufficient quantity and quality, it may prove helpful in monitoring and evaluating aspects of tire safety performance. Whether the data can eventually be used to detect the safety effects associated with differentials in specific tire design and construction characteristics such as traction is unclear. Earlier uses of these data will likely be in studies of tire structural performance, inflation pressure, and aging.

NHTSA has not established safety-related standards for tire operating characteristics, such as traction, resistance to hydroplaning, and cornering capability. Instead, the agency provides consumers with related information through the UTQG system. Tires are graded for wet traction, temperature resistance, and tread wear. However, these grades are not safety ratings, and NHTSA has not studied how they relate to tire and motor vehicle safety performance in the field.

The most recent major federal legislation covering passenger tires was the Tire Recall Enhancement, Accountability, and Documentation Act of 2000 (TREAD Act). Provisions in the act have prompted NHTSA to assess the effects of certain tire operating conditions—most notably inflation pressure—on vehicle crashes. The legislation requires the agency to mandate a tire pressure monitoring system (TPMS) in each new passenger vehicle to indicate when a tire is significantly underinflated. In support of the TPMS rulemaking, NHTSA has conducted an assessment of the benefits and costs of TPMS, in which it estimated how changes in tire traction characteristics caused by the effects of inflation pressure on a tire's footprint and stopping capability would impinge on safety. The results of the assessment are provided later in this section since they offer one quantitative indication of how tire traction characteristics and vehicle crashes may be related.

The main challenge in assessing the effect of lowering tire rolling resistance on vehicle safety is largely an empirical one. At present, there are no viable data with which to examine the safety effects of changes in tire traction. Marginal changes are difficult to discern and even more difficult to relate to crash initiations and outcomes. The one measure of traction that is available for all passenger tires is the UTQG system grade for wet traction, as described in Chapter 2. All of the passenger tires sampled for rolling resistance in the 2002 Ecos Consulting and the 2005 Rubber Manufacturers Association (RMA) data sets (presented in Chapter 3) have UTQG traction grades. These data sets are therefore analyzed below in combination. No inferences can be drawn with regard to safety relationships, but the data analyses do offer some indications of the degree of correlation between tire rolling resistance and UTQG traction. As noted in Chapter 3, there may be inconsistencies in the data derived from multiple sources (e.g., three tire companies in the case of the RMA data) and testing facilities. Nevertheless, the committee believes that the combined data sets offer greater analytical opportunity for a general investigation of possible relationships.

## UTQG Traction Grades and Rolling Resistance

Chapter 2 describes how passenger tires are tested by the UTQG system for wet traction and assigned a grade of AA, A, B, or C. NHTSA data indicate that of the 2,371 rated passenger tire lines, 4 percent are graded AA, 78 percent A, and 18 percent B or C (Table 4-1).[3] In comparison, the

---

[3] www.safercars.gov/Tires/pages/Tires2.cfm. The data are undated but presumed to be for 2004 tire models.

**TABLE 4-1** UTQG Wet Traction Grades for All Rated Tire Lines and in the Combined Ecos Consulting and RMA Data

| Traction Grade | Grade Criterion for Traction on Wet Asphalt (Measured Sliding Friction Coefficient) | Grade Criterion for Traction on Wet Concrete (Measured Sliding Friction Coefficient) | Percentage of All NHTSA-Graded Tire Lines Receiving Grade | Tires in Combined Ecos and RMA Data Receiving Grade | |
|---|---|---|---|---|---|
| | | | | Percentage | Number |
| AA | >0.54 | >0.38 | 4 | 21 | 42 |
| A | >0.47 | >0.35 | 78 | 72 | 141 |
| B | >0.38 | >0.26 | 18 | 7 | 13 |
| C | <0.38 | <0.26 | <1 | 0 | 0 |
| Total | | | 100 | 100 | 196 |

combined Ecos Consulting and RMA data contain a much larger proportion of AA-graded tires, probably because of the large percentage of high-performance tires in these samples (Table 4-1). Of the 40 tires in the combined data set having W, Y, or Z speed ratings, all but four have a grade of AA for wet traction. Only six other tires, including only one S- or T-rated tire, have a grade of AA. However, neither the NHTSA percentages nor the percentages in the combined data set are sales weighted; hence, which distribution of UTQG grades is more representative of tires found on the road is unknown.

The utility of the UTQG traction grades for exploring possible relationships with other tire characteristics such as rolling resistance is diminished by the wide range of friction coefficients within each grade, which leads to a preponderance of tires across a wide array of sizes and types receiving a grade of A. Without access to the measured friction coefficients underlying the grades assigned to individual tires, the relationships between traction and other characteristics cannot be established precisely.

A simple two-variable analysis can help describe the data. Figure 4-1 shows that tires with higher wet traction grades tend to have higher RRCs. At the same time, the graph reveals a wide spread in RRCs within all three grades. More than one-quarter of the AA-graded tires have RRCs below 0.010, and one-quarter have values above 0.012. Not found

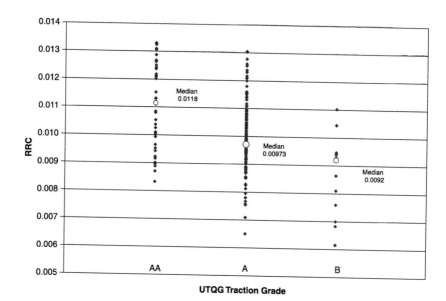

**FIGURE 4-1**  RRCs by UTQG wet traction grade, combined Ecos and RMA data.

among the AA-graded tires are very low RRCs; none of these tires has an RRC lower than 0.008. The absence of very low RRCs among AA-graded tires may indicate a lack of consumer demand for energy performance in high-traction tires, or it may be indicative of a technical or cost difficulty in achieving both qualities. The RRCs for A-graded tires cover a wider spectrum, from a low of 0.0065 to a high of 0.013. The wide spread suggests the technical feasibility of achieving both low rolling resistance and A levels of wet traction, although the production cost implications of doing so are not evident from the data.

As reported in Chapter 3, RRCs tend to decline as rim diameter increases. Thus, whether achieving a low RRC and a wet traction grade of A is more difficult for tires designed for 13-, 14-, and 15-inch rims than it is for tires with larger rim diameters would be useful to determine. Figure 4-2 suggests that low RRCs are less common among the smaller tires with an A traction grade. Only three of the 76 tires with 13-, 14-, and 15-inch rim diameters have an RRC lower than 0.008, and only one of the three received an A traction grade, as shown in Figure 4-2.

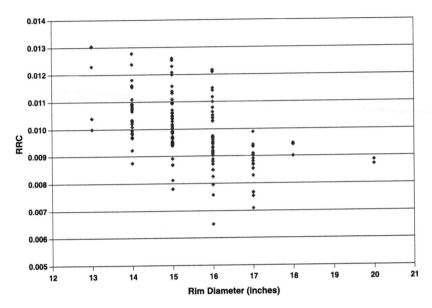

**FIGURE 4-2** RRCs for tires with a UTQG grade of A for wet traction, sorted by rim diameter (combined Ecos and RMA data).

Although the statistical analyses do suggest a relationship, characterizing traction as negatively related to rolling resistance on the basis of these data alone would be an oversimplification. There is a wide spread in RRCs within all three traction grades. RRCs below 0.01 are found among all traction grades, and more than 25 percent of the highest-traction (AA) tires in the combined data have such RRCs (Figure 4-1).

In summary, the data suggest the difficulty of achieving both an AA traction grade and very low rolling resistance, even among tires having larger rim diameters in the current market. They do not, however, reveal the cost implications or the technological requirements, such as changes in tire design or materials, of achieving such an outcome.

## Safety Implications of Traction Differentials

As explained earlier, the UTQG system is of limited usefulness in judging tire traction characteristics. The four-letter classification in the grading system results in large numbers of tires receiving the same grade, and marginal differences in traction that may exist among tires graded the same are difficult to observe. In addition, the sliding friction coefficients used to derive the grades are measured under a limited set of operating conditions (locked-wheel, straight-line braking on either of the two wet pavements at one speed). Thus the coefficients do not indicate traction characteristics under a range of speeds or under common operating conditions such as travel on dry surfaces, cornering, and antilock braking. Moreover, the UTQG test does not take into account the drainage characteristics of the tire's tread pattern, which may affect susceptibility to hydroplaning as well as wet traction.

One cause of the UTQG limitations is that the traction grades were developed not to provide comprehensive tire safety assessments but rather to provide consumers with more information on one aspect of tire performance relevant in making purchase decisions. If more precise metrics on tire traction were available, the effects of modifications in tire designs and materials to reduce rolling resistance on this particular characteristic might be explored further. Whether more precise traction data would, in turn, permit the examination of subsequent effects on vehicle safety performance is an open question.

The factors that influence the incidence and severity of motor vehicle crashes, such as the behavior of the driver and the condition of the vehicle and operating environment, are many and complex. Only rarely does analysis point to a single factor, especially a factor as difficult to measure and quantify by one number as tire traction. It is of interest that passenger tires with a wet traction grade of AA—which are disproportionately tires with speed ratings of W, Y, or Z—are more likely to be used on high-performance sports cars than are tires with A or B traction grades.

Few studies associating tire traction and crash incidence and severity have been undertaken. As described in Box 4-1, NHTSA has recently calculated the safety effects of improved vehicle stopping distances resulting from the proper maintenance of tire inflation, which affects a tire's traction footprint. These estimates in support of regulation provide some indication of how traction capabilities may affect motor vehicle safety. However, they are too general for use in estimating the safety effects result-

---

BOX 4-1

## NHTSA Evaluation of Safety Effects of Improved Traction from TPMS

As part of its assessment of TPMS, NHTSA quantified expected reductions in crashes associated with improvements in tire traction stemming from maintenance of proper inflation. The agency estimated that if the occurrence of underinflated tires was curbed by TPMS, the average stopping distance for all injury crash–involved cars and light trucks would decline by about 1.5 percent, equivalent to what would be achieved by increasing the tire–road friction coefficient by 1.5 percent (NHTSA 2005, V-22).* Quicker braking deceleration would prevent some crashes and reduce the severity of others by lowering impact velocities. The agency estimated that each 1 percent reduction in stopping distance would prevent 25 to 30 fatalities, 130 to 140 severe injuries, and 2,300 to 2,500 moderate and slight injuries (NHTSA 2005, Table V-22).**

*In its calculations, NHTSA refers to a smaller (1.37 percent) change in *average* stopping distance by adjusting the 1.52 percent average downward by 10 percent, on the basis of an assumption that only 90 percent of drivers will pay attention to the TPMS warning and properly inflate their tires. The committee normalized the results to 1 percent increments.

**Again, the actual estimates of crash savings from traction improvements given in NHTSA's TPMS study are adjusted downward by 10 percent because of an assumed compliance rate of 90 percent.

---

ing from changes in tire designs and materials specifically to reduce average rolling resistance.

The present study was not undertaken to assess the effects—safety or otherwise—of replacement tires achieving very low or atypical levels of rolling resistance. "Low" is a relative term. Differentials of 25 percent or more in RRCs can be found today among replacement tires having the same UTQG traction grades and other characteristics. Narrowing the range of rolling resistance among tires within the same traction grades, perhaps by targeting the highest-rolling-resistance tires in the group, is one potentially benign way (with respect to traction and perhaps safety) to lower average rolling resistance. In other words, reducing the average energy loss from tires can be brought about by various means, not simply by reducing rolling resistance in all tires by the same amount.

## EFFECTS ON TREAD LIFE AND SCRAP TIRES

Scrap tires are a significant component of the nation's solid waste stream. Much progress has been made during the past two decades in finding uses for scrap tires that reduce landfill disposals and open stockpiles and thus in lowering risks from fire and insect-borne diseases.[4] Concerns related to scrap tires and the progress and challenges in controlling scrap tire generation are explained in Box 4-2. Today, more than three-quarters of all scrap tires generated each year are recovered or recycled. However, new recycling opportunities are needed because more tires are discarded each year by the nation's expanding fleet of motor vehicles.

The mass introduction of longer-wearing radial-ply tires during the 1970s and 1980s may have helped control the population of scrap tires in relation to the large growth in car ownership and vehicle travel. Radial-ply tires are not as amenable to retreading as bias-ply tires, but they last much longer. Passenger car and light truck travel has grown by an average of 1 to 3 percent per year during the past 25 years. Without additional gains in tire life, further increases in scrap tire generation can be expected, and commensurate growth in recycling and recovery capabilities will be required.

Tread wear is the main cause of tire replacement. A review of discarded tire samples by Michelin revealed that tread wear, both normal and abnormal, accounts for between two-thirds and three-quarters of discarded tires.[5] Factors affecting tread wear and life span are therefore important not only from the standpoint of the motorist, who must buy tires more often if they wear out sooner, but also from the standpoint of society's interest in controlling scrap tire populations.

---

[4] See RMA (2005) and Isayev and Oh (2005) for an overview of recycling methods and progress.
[5] See www.ciwmb.ca.gov/agendas/mtgdocs/2003/09/00012525.ppt.

BOX 4-2

## Scrap Tire Recycling Progress and Challenges

During the past two decades, states have become heavily involved in regulating scrap tires and in developing markets for them. In 1985, Minnesota became the first state to pass legislation governing many aspects of scrap tire storage, collection, processing, and use. Since then, most states have established scrap tire programs aimed at controlling disposal, encouraging recycling and reprocessing, abating stockpiles, and reducing the generation of scrap tires. Some typical features of state programs are (*a*) licensing or registration requirements for scrap tire haulers, processors, and some end users; (*b*) manifests for scrap tire shipments and controls concerning who can handle scrap tires; (*c*) financial assurance requirements for scrap tire handlers, storage facilities, and disposers; (*d*) market development activities for recycling and processing; and (*e*) tire pile cleanup programs. To help offset the cost of these programs, most states impose fees on purchases of new tires and removal of used tires.

The three largest uses for scrap tires are in tire-derived fuel, civil engineering applications, and ground rubber applications. The most common uses of tire-derived fuel are in the production of cement, in pulp and paper mills, and in the generation of electricity. The civil engineering market encompasses a wide range of uses for scrap tires, such as leachate liner, backfill, septic field drainage, and road base material. The tires are usually shredded for these applications, and a considerable amount of the tire shreds come from stockpile abatement projects. Applications of ground rubber, sometimes called crumb rubber, include the production of sheet and molded rubber products (such as floor mats and truck bed liners), new tires, and sports floor surfacing.

*(continued on next page)*

BOX 4-2 *(continued)*
**Scrap Tire Recycling Progress and Challenges**

Some states—most notably Arizona, Florida, and California—use ground tire rubber to produce asphalt binder, pavement sealers, and substitutes for aggregate in pavements. The cost of transporting scrap tires, especially in rural areas, can be a significant obstacle in finding economical markets for both newly generated and stockpiled scrap tires. Many scrap tire applications are low-value and low-margin uses. They are subject to fluctuations in market demand that hinge on the availability of substitute products and macroeconomic conditions, such as the price of energy. To keep scrap tire markets growing, many states have taken an active role in developing markets and in using scrap tires themselves in highway construction and other civil engineering projects. Some also support research to assess the environmental effects of using tires in various ways, including analyses of emissions from tire-derived fuels, leaching from tires used as fill, and the disposition of residue from tire processing.

According to RMA data, 130 million of the 290 million scrap tires generated in 2003 were reused as tire-derived fuel in various industrial facilities and about 100 million were recycled into new products (RMA 2005, 48). Of the remaining 60 million tires, about half were buried in landfills and the other half are unaccounted for.* In addition to these newly generated tires, about 275 million scrap tires have accumulated in stockpiles across the country. Four states—Texas, Colorado, Michigan, and New York—accounted for about half this total, which has been reduced considerably during the past decade. The U.S. Environ-

---

* Unaccounted-for tires may result from overestimation of generation numbers; inaccurate or incomplete reporting by tire sales, disposal, and processing facilities; unrecorded uses such as tarp weights at farms and tires remaining on junked vehicles; and tires that are illegally dumped.

mental Protection Agency has estimated that more than 700 million scrap tires were stockpiled 10 years ago. The scrap tires in long-standing stockpiles have fewer uses than cleaner, newly generated tires because of their poorer condition and limited accessibility. Nevertheless, the abatement of these stockpiles adds supply to the scrap tire markets, which complicates efforts to find economical uses for the millions of new scrap tires generated each year.

## UTQG Tread Wear Grades and Rolling Resistance

Tires are rated for tread wear as part of UTQG. As discussed in Chapter 2, these grades are numerical, and most assigned values range from 100 to 800. The scale is an index intended to reflect relative wear life. In general, tires graded 400 should outwear tires graded 200. Whether tires rated 400 wear twice as long, *on average*, as tires rated 200 is unknown, since there have been no follow-up examinations of average tire wear experience in the field and how this compares with UTQG ratings. The test is conducted on an outdoor track under controlled conditions. Both NHTSA and tire manufacturers warn against assuming that an individual tire will achieve wear performance proportional to its rating, because tires can be subject to different applications and operating environments. Nevertheless, some proportional relationship, on the average for large numbers of tires, is implied by the numerical design of the rating system.

Table 4-2 compares the UTQG tread wear grades of the new tires in the combined Ecos Consulting and RMA data with the grades received by all passenger tire lines reported by NHTSA. A larger percentage of tires in the combined data have very high tread wear ratings, and a smaller percentage have very low ratings. More than half of the tires in the combined data set have a rating between 300 and 500, which is comparable with national levels reported by NHTSA. The average tread

**TABLE 4-2** Comparison of UTQG System Grades for All Passenger Tires and for the Tires in the Combined Ecos Consulting and RMA Data

| UTQG Tread Wear Rating | Percentage of All Tires with Grade According to NHTSA | Tires in Combined Ecos Consulting and RMA Data | |
|---|---|---|---|
| | | Percentage | Number |
| 200 or less | 11 | 3 | 6 |
| 201–300 | 21 | 18 | 36 |
| 301–400 | 33 | 28 | 55 |
| 401–500 | 22 | 23 | 45 |
| 501–600 | 8 | 17 | 33 |
| 601 or more | 5 | 11 | 21 |
| Total | 100 | 100 | 196 |

wear grade for the data set is 440. As noted previously, neither the combined data nor NHTSA's national ratings are sales weighted. Therefore, neither can be used to calculate an average UTQG wear rating for all tires sold.

A scatter graph of all 196 tires in the combined data set does not exhibit any noticeable association between RRC and tread wear rating, as shown in Figure 4-3a. Disaggregating the data by graphing only the tires in the data set rated S or T reveals a slightly noticeable, but still weak, pattern (Figure 4-3b). Further disaggregation by graphing only those S or T tires with 15-inch rim diameters (Figure 4-3c) suggests the possibility of a relationship between rolling resistance and UTQG tread wear grade, which warrants more data for thorough statistical analysis involving more explanatory variables.

## Explaining Variability in RRC and Tread Wear Grades

Multivariate analysis can help determine whether there is a relationship between RRC and UTQG tread wear rating and other variables among the 196 tires in the combined data. The original variables in the data set are

- RRC,
- Speed rating (S, T; H, V; W, Y, Z),
- Tire manufacturer,

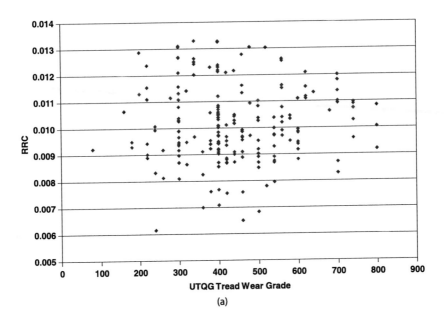

(a)

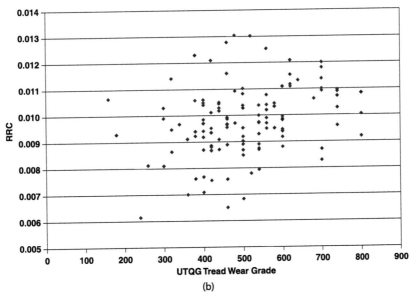

(b)

**FIGURE 4-3**  Scatter graphs of RRC and UTQG tread wear ratings, combined data set: (*a*) all 196 tires; (*b*) tires with speed rating of S or T.

*(continued on next page)*

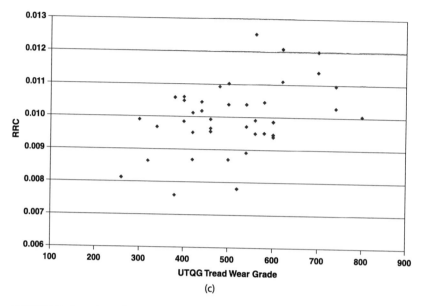

FIGURE 4-3 *(continued)* Scatter graphs of RRC and UTQG tread wear ratings, combined data set: *(c)* tires with speed rating of S or T and 15-inch rim diameter.

- Aspect ratio,
- Rim diameter (inches),
- UTQG temperature grade (A, B, C),
- UTQG traction grade (AA, A, B),
- UTQG tread wear rating, and
- Market [replacement or original equipment (OE)].

The committee added data for the following three variables:

- Tread depth,
- Retail price, and
- Tire weight.

Tread depth and tire weight were obtained from the catalogue of tire specifications accessible on each tire manufacturer's website. Tread depth was found for 170 of the 196 tires in the sample, and tire weight was found for all but six of the tires. The former is a measure of the depth of the tread grooves and thus excludes the tread base. Retail prices were established for each of the tires from Internet searches of several popular tire mail order sites, including www.Tirerack.com (price sources are noted in the data table). The price data are examined in Chapter 5.

As noted in Chapter 1, because the RMA data did not become available until late in this study, a limited number of statistical analyses and tests could be performed on the data. Multiple regression models were tested with RRC as the dependent variable and combinations of the other variables listed above as independent variables. RRC is expressed as a natural logarithm to provide a better model fit and to allow for interpretations of the regression coefficients in terms of percentage change. Some of the categoric variables (e.g., speed rating, manufacturer, traction grade) are included as dummy variables.[6] The results of the two best-fitting regression models are presented below.[7] The first model seeks to explain variability in RRC. The second seeks to explain variability in UTQG tread wear rating. The implications of the results of the two models are discussed later.

### Explaining Variability in RRC

Table 4-3 gives the results of a model explaining the natural logarithm of RRC as a function of tire rim diameter, aspect ratio, and tread depth, as well as dummy variables for tires having a speed rating of W, Y, or Z (hispeed), H or V (midspeed), and a UTQG traction grade of B (tractionB). Dummies were also created for tires made by Michelin and for those observations from the Ecos Consulting (ecosdummy) data set.[8] All independent variables, except ecosdummy, are significant at the 95 percent confidence level, and the model statistically explains about half the variation observed in RRC, as indicated by the adjusted $R^2$ of 0.50.

---

[6] A dummy variable is a numerical variable used in regression analysis to represent subgroups of the observations in the sample.

[7] With 10 independent variables to choose among, it is possible to test more than 2,000 models by using combinations of one or more independent variables. The committee therefore focused on variables that are most indicative of the engineering parameters that tire manufacturers can affect to achieve properties such as lower rolling resistance and higher tread wear resistance.

[8] Because ecosdummy was statistically significant at the 90 percent level, it was left in the model.

**TABLE 4-3** Output of Multiple Regression: RRC (Natural Logarithm) as a Function of Eight Independent Variables

| | Coeff. | Std. Error | t | 95% Confidence Range | |
|---|---|---|---|---|---|
| | | | | Lower Limit | Upper Limit |
| hispeed | .160 | .030 | 5.4 | .102 | .221 |
| midspeed | .047 | .020 | 2.3 | .007 | .098 |
| michelin | −.064 | .020 | −3.2 | −.104 | −.025 |
| rimdiameter | −.066 | .007 | −9.3 | −.081 | −.053 |
| aspectratio | −.009 | .002 | −6.3 | −.012 | −.006 |
| treaddepth | .042 | .009 | 4.9 | .025 | .060 |
| tractionB | −.120 | .036 | −3.3 | −.192 | −.048 |
| ecosdummy | −.044 | .024 | −1.8 | −.094 | .005 |

NOTE: Number of observations = 170; $R^2$ = .52; adjusted $R^2$ = .50.

Under the assumption that all other variables are held constant, the regression coefficients and their confidence intervals indicate each variable's relationship with RRC. The results are consistent with the findings in Chapter 3 that, on average, RRC declines as rim diameter increases and that RRC increases with higher speed ratings.

The results indicate that increasing rim diameter by 1 inch, or about 6.3 percent for the average tire in the data set, reduces RRC by 5 to 8 percent. Compared with tires with lower speed ratings (S, T), tires with the highest speed ratings (W, Y, Z) have 10 to 22 percent higher RRCs, while tires with middle speed ratings (H, V) have 1 to 9 percent higher RRCs.

Tires with thicker tread tend to have higher RRCs. Tread depth is measured and reported in increments of 1/32 inch, and an increase of one unit, or 1/32 inch, leads to a 2.5 to 6 percent increase in RRC, with a midpoint of 4.3 percent. An increase of 1/32 inch is an approximate increase in tread depth of 9 percent for the average tire in the data set. These results imply that to obtain a 10 percent reduction in RRC, an average tire's tread depth would need to decrease by about 22 percent.

The relationship between RRC and traction is more difficult to explore because most tires are graded A for UTQG wet traction (out of a possible AA, A, or B), which is indicative of the broad band of grades in this rating scheme. Nevertheless, the dozen or so tires in the data set with a B grade have a 5 to 19 percent lower RRC than all other tires, all else being equal.

Variables not included in the model are tire weight and dummies for UTQG temperature grade, neither of which was found to be statistically significant. Retail price was not included in the model, since it is not a parameter that can be changed directly to affect RRC in the same manner as a physical property.[9] Nevertheless, to the extent that tire prices reflect tire manufacturing costs, price is an important consideration. Analyses of the selling prices of tires in the combined data set are presented in Chapter 5.

A dummy for OE tires was tested, but the small number (eight) of OE tires in the data set limited its significance. The data set consists almost entirely of replacement tires. To the degree that OE tires are constructed on the basis of technologies not common in replacement tires—for instance, by using alternative tread compounds to reduce rolling resistance—the kinds of relationships reported in Table 4-3 might not emerge from an analysis of large numbers of OE tires. Whether differences exist in OE and replacement tire technologies is an open question that is considered further in Chapter 5.

### Explaining Variability in UTQG Tread Wear Rating

Table 4-4 shows the results of a regression explaining UTQG tread wear rating as a function of six variables. Once again, speed rating is a highly significant variable; tires rated for higher speeds tend to have lower tread wear grades. Compared with all other tires in the data set, tires with a speed rating of W, Y, or Z have average tread wear ratings that are 175 to 275 points lower. Tread wear ratings of tires having speed ratings of H or V are lower by 50 to 130 points.

As might be expected, there is also a statistical relationship between a tire's tread wear rating and tread depth. The regression coefficient indicates that each increase of 1/32 inch in tread depth results in a 1- to 39-point increase in the tread wear rating, with a midpoint of about 20.

---

[9] It is inappropriate to include price as a regressor in the RRC regression because it is not a predetermined variable and would thus bias the results.

**TABLE 4-4** Output of Multiple Regression Performed on Combined Data Set Explaining UTQG Tread Wear Rating as a Function of Six Variables

| | Coeff. | Std. Error | t | 95% Confidence Range | |
| | | | | Lower Limit | Upper Limit |
|---|---|---|---|---|---|
| treaddepth | 20.1 | 9.6 | 2.1 | 1.1 | 39.0 |
| tireweight | −5.6 | 1.3 | −4.2 | −8.3 | −3.0 |
| midspeed | −89.6 | 20.0 | −4.5 | −129.1 | −50.1 |
| hispeed | −227.2 | 24.3 | −9.4 | −275.3 | −179.2 |
| michelin | 48.2 | 20.2 | 2.4 | 8.3 | 88.1 |
| tractionB | −107.4 | 41.6 | −2.6 | −189.5 | −25.2 |

NOTE: Number of observations = 164; $R^2$ = .51; adjusted $R^2$ = .50.

The difference between the lowest and highest tread depths in the data set is 4/32 inch (the range is 9/32 to 13/32 inch, excluding two outliers). Hence, as a general approximation, a 2/32-inch change in tread depth would result in a change in UTQG of ±40 points, or about 10 percent for a tire having the average grade of 440 observed in the combined data set.

### Regression Results with Respect to Tread Life

While these statistical analyses are not substitutes for experimental investigations of engineering relationships, they provide insights that are difficult to observe from experiments. Experimental investigations are often limited to changing a few design or operating parameters at a time. They can be cumbersome and costly to perform because of the many factors influencing rolling resistance. The multiple regression results are consistent with findings from previous experimental studies showing that RRC can be lowered by reducing tread depth, as discussed in Chapter 3.[10] The overall results indicate that tread depth must be reduced by slightly more than 2/32 inch to achieve a 10 percent reduction in RRC, if tread reduction is the only change made. This would amount to an

---

[10] In particular, a review of the technical literature by Schuring (1980) finds that RRC is reduced by 20 to 40 percent as tread depth diminishes over a tire's wear life.

18 percent reduction in tread depth for the average tire in the combined data set.

A relationship between a new tire's tread depth and its anticipated tread life is suggested, although it was not tested directly. The UTQG tread wear ratings were developed to provide consumers with an indication of expected tread life. The ratings, however, cannot be translated into a specific number of miles of expected wear. The regression results do show that reductions in UTQG tread wear ratings are explained in part by lower tread depth. The 18 percent reduction in tread depth (about 2/32 inch) required to achieve an approximate 10 percent reduction in RRC would lead to a 10 percent reduction in the UTQG tread wear rating for the average tire.

Reducing hysteretic tread material is one approach to reducing rolling resistance. This raises the question of whether such an approach, if widely applied, would have an adverse effect on tread wear and average tire life. The data, however, do not indicate the combination of means by which tire manufacturers would lower the rolling resistance of new tires, nor do they indicate whether consumers would accept tires with lower rolling resistance if their wear lives were shortened. This simplified approach relates only to the single dimension of tread depth. In practice, tire designers could minimize tread volume and mass by reducing tread width, shoulder profile, and section width in order to affect rolling resistance while minimizing losses in wear life.

Reducing tread may achieve a lower RRC value at the outset of a tire's life, but it may not translate into a significant reduction in rolling resistance over the tire's entire life. A tire starting out with a thicker tread will eventually assume a wear profile similar to that of an otherwise comparable tire starting out with less tread. Because all tires exhibit lower rolling resistance as they wear, a tire starting out with more tread will have higher rolling resistance only until the tread wears down to the starting depth of the thinner-treaded tire. If consumers replace their tires at the same wear depth (e.g., 2/32 inch), the differential in *average* lifetime rolling resistance of the two tires should be less than the differential in the tires' RRCs measured when both tires are new.

New technologies may improve tire energy performance without the need to sacrifice tread wear or other desired capabilities. Examples of technologies developed with these goals in mind are given in Chapter 5.

## Environmental Implications of Changes in Tread Life

Tread life is important to motorists, since it affects the service life of tires and the frequency of replacement tire purchases. It is also important from the standpoint of environmental policy because of concerns with regard to scrap tire generation and disposal.

From 1970 to 2003, the number of passenger cars and light trucks in the U.S. fleet more than doubled and total vehicle miles traveled grew by more than 130 percent (FHWA 1995, Table VM-201; FHWA 2003, Table VM-201). The number of tires sold (for both OE and replacement uses) went up at a much slower rate, by 48 percent—from 167 million to 250 million tires. A plausible cause of this marked differential in trends is that passenger tires became much more durable and longer lasting after the mass introduction of radial-ply tires during the 1970s and 1980s. Even though radial tires are not as amenable to retreading, they last twice as long as the bias-ply tires they replaced.

Had these substantial gains in tire life not occurred, many additional tires would have been sold to U.S. motorists in 2003—probably about 100 million more, absent a significant increase in bias-ply retreading. Additional tires would have been sold during the two preceding decades as well. The additional tires would have been accompanied by a comparable increase in the number of scrap tires entering the waste and recycling streams. The gains in tire life attributable to radial-ply construction are an example of technological progress. Yet even as average tire life has been extended, the constantly expanding fleet of passenger vehicles and increases in vehicle travel have resulted in increasing numbers of tires being sold. Fifty million more passenger tires are shipped in the OE and replacement markets today than were shipped in 1990 (RMA 2005).

Much progress has been made during the past two decades in finding new methods of recycling scrap tires. Productive uses of scrap tires and the efforts of states and private industry to promote recycling and reuse are described in Box 4-2. In 1990, only about 11 percent of scrap tires generated were recovered or recycled, compared with more than 80 percent today (RMA 2005). Nevertheless, many states, such as Pennsylvania and California, remain concerned that trends in motor vehicle travel will lead to growing numbers of scrap tires that will overwhelm recycling markets. They have therefore started promoting ways to reduce the rate of scrap tire generation. For example, they urge motorists to buy tires promising longer tread wear and to be more vigilant with regard to tire maintenance. States (as well as the U.S. Environmental Protection Agency) are also paying attention to trends in the tire marketplace that can affect average tire life.

Some simple calculations illustrate the challenge inherent in controlling scrap tires in the face of 1 to 3 percent annual growth in motor vehicle travel. In 1995, each passenger car in the U.S. fleet averaged about 11,000 miles per year (FHWA 1995, Table VM-1). Accordingly, a set of four tires averaging 45,000 miles of service life needed to be replaced every 4.09 years. This replacement activity generated an average of 0.98 scrap tires each year for each of the 198 million passenger cars in the fleet at that time, or about 194 million scrap passenger tires nationally. By 2003, average miles driven per passenger car had increased to 12,000 miles (FHWA 2003, Table VM-1). Hence, a comparable set of tires would need to be replaced every 3.75 years, which would generate 1.07 scrap tires per year for each of the 220 million passenger vehicles in the fleet, or about 235 million scrap passenger tires nationally. Under these circumstances of increasing motor vehicle use, average tire life would need to have increased by more than 20 percent just to keep the annual generation of scrap tires constant at 1995 levels.

While holding scrap tire populations constant at earlier levels may be unrealistic, these rough calculations illustrate the importance of continued progress in extending tire life. If efforts to reduce rolling resistance raise the possibility of even modest adverse effects on tire life, the collective outcome may be problematic with regard to tire recycling and disposal. Of course, the same challenge may emerge as a result of other trends in tire design and construction that can affect tire life, such as growth in the use of tires rated for higher speeds, which are associated with shorter wear life.

## SUMMARY

Tire energy performance, traction, and wear life are related primarily because of their association with the tire's design and construction, and especially its tread. Deformation of the tread accounts for much of the hysteretic energy losses from a tire exhibiting rolling resistance. The tread's main operating function is to provide traction, especially in wet and snow conditions. The gradual loss of traction capability as the tread wears is a main determinant of a tire's service life.

Statistical analyses of sampled replacement tires suggest that most tires having high (AAA) UTQG wet traction grades are rated for high speeds and that few such tires attain low levels of rolling resistance. These results may reflect the technical difficulty of designing tires that can achieve high levels of wet traction and low rolling resistance. They may also reflect a lack of interest in energy performance among users and makers of high-performance tires or a general lack of consumer information on this characteristic. Among the majority of tires that have an A grade for wet traction, the spread in RRCs is much wider. Indeed, the existence of numerous tires having both low RRCs and an A grade for wet traction suggests the potential to reduce rolling resistance in some tires while maintaining the most common traction capability as measured by UTQG. RRC differentials of 20 percent or more can be found among tires of the same size, speed rating, and UTQG traction grade.

The RRC of new tires can be lowered by reducing tread volume and mass, among other possible means. Experimental studies indicate that a new tire's rolling resistance typically declines by 20 percent or more as the tread diminishes to its worn-out depth, a loss that may exceed 8/32 inch. The statistical analyses presented in this chapter yield results that are consistent with those of these previous studies. They indicate that reducing tread pattern depth in new tires by 18 percent, or about 2/32 inch, is associated with a 10 percent reduction in the RRC (again, measured when the tires are new). At the same time, a reduction in new-tire tread depth of 2/32 inch is associated with roughly a 10 percent reduction in the UTQG wear grade for an average tire in the data set.

Reducing a tire's RRC when it is new may not appreciably reduce its average RRC over its lifetime. A reduction in tread depth that lowers initial RRC may translate into a much smaller reduction in rolling resistance measured over a tire's full lifetime of use, which will limit the energy savings. The reason is that all tires experience diminished rolling resistance with wear; hence, a tire with thicker tread will have higher rolling resistance only until the added tread wears down to the tread depth of the thinner-treaded tire. At the same time, the likelihood of shorter wear life for tires designed with reduced tread depth or with less wear resistance for any other reason works against controlling the growth in scrap tires caused by escalating motor vehicle travel. The potential for such adverse outcomes suggests the importance of exploring means of reducing tire rolling resistance that do not degrade wear life.

## REFERENCES

### Abbreviations

FHWA    Federal Highway Administration
NHTSA   National Highway Traffic Safety Administration
RMA     Rubber Manufacturers Association

FHWA. 1995. *Highway Statistics*. U.S. Department of Transportation, Washington, D.C.

FHWA. 2003. *Highway Statistics*. U.S. Department of Transportation, Washington, D.C.

French, T. 1989. *Tyre Technology*. Adam Hilger, Bristol, England.

Gardner, J. D., and B. J. Queiser. 2005. Introduction to Tire Safety, Durability, and Failure Analysis. In *The Pneumatic Tire* (J. D. Walter and A. N. Gent, eds.), National Highway Traffic Safety Administration, Washington, D.C., pp. 612–640.

Isayev, A. I., and J. S. Oh. 2005. Tire Materials: Recovery and Re-Use. In *The Pneumatic Tire* (J. D. Walter and A. N. Gent, eds.), National Highway Traffic Safety Administration, Washington, D.C., pp. 670–693.

NHTSA. 2005. *Tire Pressure Monitoring System FMVSS No. 138: Final Economic Assessment*. Office of Regulatory Analysis and Evaluation, National Center for Statistics and Analysis, Washington, D.C., March.

Pottinger, M. G. 2005. Forces and Moments. In *The Pneumatic Tire* (J. D. Walter and A. N. Gent, eds.), National Highway Traffic Safety Administration, Washington, D.C., pp. 286–363.

RMA. 2005. *Factbook 2005: U.S. Tire Shipment Activity Report for Statistical Year 2004.* Washington, D.C.

Schuring, D. J. 1980. The Rolling Loss of Pneumatic Tires. *Rubber Chemistry and Technology,* Vol. 53, No. 3, pp. 600–727.

Walter, J. D. 2005. Tire Properties That Affect Vehicle Steady-State Handling Behavior. In *The Pneumatic Tire* (J. D. Walter and A. N. Gent, eds.), National Highway Traffic Safety Administration, Washington, D.C., pp. 594–611.

# 5

# National Consumer Savings and Costs

Congress asked that this study "address the cost to the consumer, including the additional cost of replacement tires and any potential fuel savings" associated with low-rolling-resistance tires. Congress did not define "low" rolling resistance, and the data examined show a wide range of rolling resistance values among passenger tires currently being sold in the replacement market. These measured rolling resistance values pertain to new tires. The actual rolling resistance of passenger tires averaged over a lifetime of use would be more relevant. The approach taken in this chapter, therefore, is to approximate the savings and costs to consumers if the average rolling resistance of replacement tires used on passenger vehicles were to decline by a given amount. In particular, consideration is given to what would happen to consumer expenditures on motor fuel and tires if the average rolling resistance of replacement tires in the fleet were reduced by 10 percent.

No predictions are made about how or over what time period the assumed 10 percent reduction would take place. Such a change could occur in a number of ways and over various time frames. It could result in part from the development and production of more tires with lower rolling resistance and their gradual or rapid introduction into the replacement market. It could result from changes in the mix of existing makes, models, sizes, and types of tires purchased by motorists, since there is already much variability in rolling resistance among tires in the marketplace. If more tires with lower rolling resistance are purchased by consumers, the average rolling resistance of the replacement tire population would likely decline. The 10 percent reduction could also result, at least in part, from motorists taking better care of their tires, particularly through proper inflation. The occurrence of one or more of the above developments leading to a 10 percent decline in average rolling resistance is a reasonable expectation.

The monetary savings and costs to consumers of such a reduction in rolling resistance can be quantified. The two consumer expenditure items of interest to Congress are motor fuel and tires. All else being equal, a reduction in rolling resistance is certain to reduce motor fuel expenditures. At issue is how large the savings would be. Chapter 3 indicates that a 10 percent reduction in rolling resistance will cause a 1 to 2 percent reduction in fuel consumption per mile driven. The effect on tire-related expenditures is more difficult to estimate without knowing the details of how the change in rolling resistance is brought about. For example, if rolling resistance is reduced because of better tire maintenance, consumers may end up spending less on tires, because properly inflated tires will have longer wear in addition to providing better fuel economy. In contrast, if the reduction is brought about by the sale of more tires that have reduced wear life, consumers may end up spending more on tires because of the need to replace them more often.

Given the many possible ways to reduce average rolling resistance, the approach taken in this chapter is to present two plausible scenarios that illustrate the potential for impacts on tire expenditures. Under the first scenario, a greater proportion of existing tires with lower rolling resistance and a smaller proportion of existing tires with higher rolling resistance are purchased in the marketplace. Under the second, many new tire designs are introduced that achieve lower rolling resistance through changes in tire materials, particularly in tread composition.

The next section reviews how a reduction in average rolling resistance can affect consumer fuel expenditures. Most of the remainder of the chapter examines the effects on tire expenditures. The chapter concludes by considering the two consumer expenditure items together.

The estimates are developed for consumers as a whole and are presented as national annualized averages. As a group, U.S. motorists make expenditures on motor fuel and replacement tires each year. Estimates are made for how average expenditures may be affected by a reduction in replacement tire rolling resistance. From the perspective of the individual consumer, outlays on fuel and tires are made over different time horizons and in different increments. For example, a tankful of fuel is purchased about once a week and a set of tires every 3 or more years. The timing and size of these outlays are important in the calculus of individual consumers in making their own purchase decisions. Motorists will value a dollar saved or spent today more highly than one saved or spent in the future. The timing of these expenditure flows is not relevant in quantifying the effects on consumers collectively because timing differences average out. In other contexts, however, the timing of outlays is relevant, especially in considering the response of individual consumers to information on tire energy performance.

## CONSUMER FUEL SAVINGS

Chapter 3 suggests that a 10 percent reduction in average rolling resistance would translate to a 1 to 2 percent reduction in passenger vehicle fuel consumption per mile. As noted in Chapter 2, passenger vehicles in the United States are driven an average of 12,000 miles per year and consume about 600 gallons of fuel in the process. A 1 to 2 percent reduction in fuel consumption would equate to fuel savings of 6 to 12 gallons per year.[1] The U.S. Department of Energy, in its *Annual Energy Outlook 2006*, projects an average price for motor fuel of $2.02 per gallon for the next several years (EIA 2005, Table A12). On the basis of a price of $2 per gallon, the savings to motorists from using replacement tires with lower rolling resistance would be $12 to $24 per vehicle per year.

Multiplying these savings by the number of vehicles in the passenger fleet and subtracting out the share of vehicles equipped with original equipment (OE) tires results in an estimate of the collective savings to consumers.[2] Tire shipment data presented in Chapter 2 indicate that about 20 percent of tires in the fleet are OE and 80 percent are replacement.[3] Accordingly, in any given year, about 20 percent of the fleet, or about

---

[1] The calculation assumes that motorists will not drive more miles in response to increased fuel economy, which will reduce the effective fuel cost of driving (see discussion of the rebound effect in Chapter 3).

[2] See Chapters 1 and 2 for fleet data, which are derived from U.S. Department of Energy and U.S. Department of Transportation statistics.

[3] As explained in Chapter 2, OE tires account for about 20 percent of tire shipments, and replacement tires account for 80 percent. Although the exact percentages of tires in the fleet that are OE and replacement are unknown, this 20:80 ratio offers a reasonable approximation.

45 million passenger vehicles from the current fleet of 220 million,[4] would be unaffected by the 10 percent reduction in the average rolling resistance of replacement tires. The remaining 175 million passenger vehicles that are affected would consume 1 billion to 2 billion fewer gallons of fuel per year (175 million vehicles × 6 gallons to 12 gallons). Users of these vehicles would therefore save $2 billion to $4 billion per year in fuel expenditures.

These estimates assume that other characteristics of the vehicle fleet, such as size, technologies, and miles of travel, do not change. Of course, the passenger vehicle fleet will become larger over time, and vehicle technologies and average miles of travel per vehicle will change. The fuel savings are estimated without an allowance (which would be speculative) for such developments and without anticipating a time frame for the reduction in rolling resistance. This straightforward approach is also used in estimating potential effects on consumer tire expenditures.[5]

## CONSUMER TIRE EXPENDITURES

Consumer expenditures on tires are governed by (*a*) the frequency of their tire replacement and (*b*) the costs they incur during each replacement, including the tire's purchase price and related costs such as the motorist's time and money spent on tire installation. The first is affected by the tire's durability characteristics, such as tread wear resistance. Accordingly, information on the effects of reducing new-tire rolling resistance on tread wear, as examined in Chapter 4, is helpful in estimating the frequency of tire replacement. The second is affected by tire production and installation costs, as well as other factors such as the value of motorists' time. Consideration is given to these factors in the following two scenarios.

---

[4] This estimated number of in-fleet vehicles with OE tires is consistent with the number of new passenger vehicles entering the fleet over a 3-year period, after which tires are often replaced.

[5] Brief consideration was given in Chapter 3 to a consumer response to increases in vehicle fuel economy known as the "rebound effect." By effectively lowering the fuel cost of driving, an improvement in vehicle fuel economy may cause motorists to drive more, which would offset some of the total fuel savings that are anticipated from the fuel economy improvement. Studies of this consumer response suggest that about 10 percent of the expected fuel savings may be offset (Small and Van Dender 2005). This is an example of a second-order effect that is not factored into the estimates of fuel savings because it would not change the order of magnitude of the savings estimate.

## Scenario 1: Changes in Consumer Purchases of Tires Currently on the Market Lead to a Reduction in Average Rolling Resistance

The data analyzed in Chapter 3 indicate how rolling resistance can vary widely among tires, even among those that are comparable with respect to many other characteristics. Differentials in rolling resistance coefficients (RRCs) of 20 percent or more, for example, were found among new tires having the same size, traction characteristics, and speed ratings. One plausible explanation for this observed difference among otherwise comparable tires is that some are designed in ways that make them more energy efficient but that affect operating performance only minimally.

If the differences in rolling resistance were widely known, some consumers might purchase tires now on the market that possess lower rolling resistance, especially if they were persuaded that desired characteristics such as traction, handling, and wear life would not be sacrificed. Presumably, tire prices would also be an important factor in their purchase decisions. The relationship between rolling resistance and tire prices has not been examined up to this point in this report. Price data, however, were collected for the tires in the combined Ecos Consulting and Rubber Manufacturers Association (RMA) data sets. The effect on average tire prices of a change in the distribution of tires purchased to reduce average rolling resistance is considered below. This is followed by an examination of the effects on average wear life if consumers achieve the reduced rolling resistance by choosing tires built with thinner treads.

### Price Effects
The tires in the combined Ecos Consulting and RMA data have a wide range of selling prices,[6] with some lower than $50 and others exceeding $300. In Figure 5-1 tire prices are plotted against the RRCs of the tires measured when they were new. The scattered pattern suggests that prices

---

[6] Retail prices were obtained by the committee during October 2005 through searches of popular tire mail order websites, including www.tirerack.com. Prices do not include tax, shipping, balancing, mounting, or other incidentals, such as fees for scrap tire disposal and valve stem replacement, paid by tire buyers.

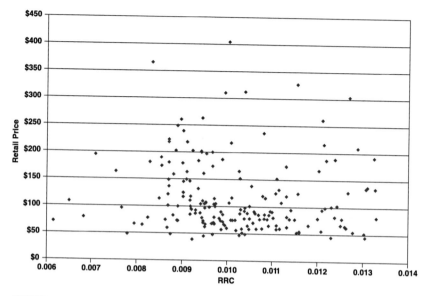

**FIGURE 5-1** Retail price versus RRC for tires in combined Ecos Consulting and RMA data.

and rolling resistance are unrelated. As explained in earlier chapters, however, the many other tire characteristics and features that can influence these patterns should be taken into account. The observed scattering of prices might be expected given the wide variety of tires in the data, encompassing dozens of combinations of sizes and speed ratings. To illustrate, Figure 5-2 shows how prices vary in relation to rim diameter and speed rating.

The pattern in Figure 5-2 reveals the importance of examining price and rolling resistance relationships for tires possessing the same size and speed ratings. Table 5-1 examines average tire prices for groups of tires having the following common rim diameters and speed ratings: 14-inch S and T, 15-inch S and T, 16-inch S and T, and 16-inch H and V. Each of these four groups contains at least 15 tires. The data are disaggregated further by the RRC of each tire.

The comparisons in Table 5-1 do not show a clear pattern of tire price differentials relating to rolling resistance. Because few new tires have RRCs below 0.009, the data reveal little about price differences among

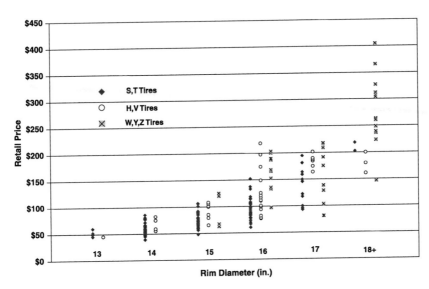

**FIGURE 5-2** Retail tire prices by rim diameter and speed rating, combined Ecos Consulting and RMA data.

tires having the lowest RRCs. Most new tires have RRCs between 0.009 and 0.011. For tires with 14- and 15-inch rim diameters, there is no obvious relationship between price and RRC. Only in the case of tires having 16-inch rim diameters is there evidence that lower rolling resistance can be accompanied by higher prices. For the S and T tires in this size group, the price differential is small and seemingly negligible. The only obvious pattern emerges among the H and V tires in the group. In this case, tires with lower RRCs tend to have higher prices, but the pattern is not unequivocal.

Several multiple regressions were also performed that sought to explain tire prices as a function of various tire characteristics. The regressions were conducted separately for tires grouped by rim diameter. The results left a substantial proportion of the variation in tire prices unexplained by the tire characteristics.

In sum, the results from empirical data do not indicate that consumers will necessarily pay more for replacement tires having lower rolling resistance.

**TABLE 5-1**  Average Tire Prices by RRC Distribution for Groupings of Tires
Having the Same Rim Size and Speed Rating, Combined Ecos Consulting
and RMA Data

| | RRC | | | | |
|---|---|---|---|---|---|
| | ≤0.008 | >0.008 to 0.009 | >0.009 to 0.01 | >0.01 to 0.011 | >0.011 |
| **14-inch S, T** | | | | | |
| Number of tires | 1 | 1 | 7 | 10 | 6 |
| Average RRC | 0.0061 | 0.0088 | 0.0097 | 0.0107 | 0.0117 |
| Average price ($) | 71.00 | 48.00 | 59.00 | 65.70 | 59.30 |
| **15-inch S, T** | | | | | |
| Number of tires | 0 | 6 | 14 | 12 | 6 |
| Average RRC | NA | 0.0085 | 0.0097 | 0.0105 | 0.0117 |
| Average price ($) | NA | 70.33 | 75.57 | 79.41 | 71.80 |
| **16-inch S, T** | | | | | |
| Number of tires | 2 | 4 | 13 | 5 | 4 |
| Average RRC | 0.0067 | 0.0087 | 0.0944 | 0.0104 | 0.0114 |
| Average price ($) | 93.50 | 102.00 | 104.00 | 102.20 | 85.25 |
| **16-inch H, V** | | | | | |
| Number of tires | 0 | 2 | 7 | 4 | 3 |
| Average RRC | NA | 0.0085 | 0.0093 | 0.0105 | 0.0117 |
| Average price ($) | NA | 113.50 | 147.00 | 113.25 | 86.00 |

NOTE: NA = not applicable. RRC values were measured when tires were new.

## Tire Wear Effects

The findings in Chapter 4 suggest that new-tire rolling resistance can be
reduced by a magnitude of 10 percent by reducing tread depth by about
22 percent. At the same time, the data suggest that tires with reduced
tread depth exhibit shorter wear life. Indeed, lower Uniform Tire Quality
Grading tread wear numerical ratings—by about 5 percent—were observed
for each 1/32-inch reduction in tread depth. This is equal to about 9 percent of tread depth for the average tire. If consumers were to purchase
more tires with less tread as the main way to achieve lower rolling resistance, they would likely experience shorter wear life and need to replace
their tires more often.

Perhaps the simplest way to approximate the effects of shorter wear
life on tire replacement expenditures is to use the figures in Chapter 2
indicating that about 200 million replacement tires are shipped in a year

for use on 175 million passenger vehicles. The ratio of vehicles to tires (175 million/200 million = 0.88) suggests that a motorist can expect to purchase a replacement tire an average of every 0.88 year, or a complete set of four tires about every 3.5 years (4 × 0.88 = 3.52).[7] If reductions in rolling resistance are brought about by consumers purchasing tires with thinner tread, the frequency of tire purchases would increase by an amount commensurate with the reduction in tire wear life.

Suppose that the average tread depth of new tires purchased decreases by 22 percent. The analyses in Chapter 4 suggest that such a change would reduce new-tire RRCs by about 10 percent and projected wear life by about 10 percent. Accordingly, the number of replacement tires purchased in a year would need to increase by about 10 percent, from 200 million to about 220 million. Motorists would thus purchase a new tire on average every 0.80 year (175 million/220 million), or a complete set of four tires every 3.2 years. In terms of annual tire expenditures, the motorist would purchase an average of 1.25 tires per year (4/3.2), as opposed to the current average of 1.14 tires per year (4/3.5).

The full cost to the consumer of having to buy an average of 0.11 more tires per year will depend on tire prices and other tire transaction and installation costs. The average price of tires in the combined Ecos Consulting and RMA data is $117. The data set, however, contains a large number of high-performance tires. While tires rated for higher speed (H, V, W, Y, Z) are becoming more popular among U.S. motorists, they do not represent 40 percent of replacement tires sales, which is their percentage in the data set. RMA's *Factbook 2005* indicates that tires rated S and T accounted for 73 percent of replacement tire shipments in 2004, while performance (H, V) and high-performance (W, Y, Z) tires accounted for 22 and 4 percent, respectively (RMA 2005, 22). Weighting the price data by these reported sales percentages suggests an average tire price of $97. Hence, consumer expenditures on tires would increase from an average of $110.58 per year (1.14 × $97) to an average of $121.25 (1.25 × $97) per year, a difference of $10.67.

---

[7] If vehicles are driven an average of 12,000 miles, this figure equates to an average tire life of 42,000 miles (3.5 years × 12,000 miles).

Other costs associated with tire replacement include the expense of installation and the inconvenience and time lost to motorists. These costs are real but difficult to quantify fully. Tire installation (e.g., balancing, mounting, and valve stem replacement) and other associated consumer expenses such as tire disposal fees can vary from $40 to more than $100 for a set of four tires, with $50 (or $12.50 per tire) being the reported average.[8] Thus, including these installation costs would add about $1.38 (0.11 × $12.50) to annual tire expenditures, which would bring the total to about $12 more per year ($10.67 + $1.38).

For the 175 million passenger vehicles using replacement tires, the total tire expenditure increase under this scenario would be $2.1 billion per year. In reality, the scenario's assumption that reduction in tread depth will be the exclusive means of achieving lower rolling resistance is questionable. Tire manufacturers can minimize tread volume and mass by means other than, or in addition to, reducing depth. For instance, tread width, shoulder profile, and section width can be modified to reduce rolling resistance while seeking to minimize adverse effects on wear life. U.S. motorists are known to demand long wear life when they purchase tires, as reflected by the mileage warranties advertised by tire companies. It is improbable that tire manufacturers interested in maintaining customers would sacrifice wear life to any major degree.

In any event, as pointed out earlier, achieving a lower RRC only by reducing tread thickness may not lead to significantly lower rolling resistance on the average over a tire's lifetime. As it accumulates miles, a tire with thicker tread will soon assume wear and rolling resistance profiles similar to those of an otherwise comparable tire starting out with thinner tread. The fuel savings will occur only during the miles driven before the added tread thickness wears down, if both tires are replaced at the same level of tread wear, and will be limited accordingly. To illustrate with a simplified example, suppose that all tires wear evenly at a rate of 1/32 inch of tread per 5,000 miles and are replaced when tread depth reaches 2/32 inch. Further, suppose that RRC declines evenly by 0.005 per 1/32 inch of tread loss, that one tire starts out with a tread depth of 10/32 inch and an RRC

---

[8] Modern Tire Dealer (2006) reports that the average customer expenditure on new-tire mounting and balancing is $49.

of 0.01, and that another starts out with a tread depth of 12/32 inch and an RRC of 0.011. The former tire's average RRC over its 40,000-mile lifetime will be 0.00825, while the latter tire's average RRC over its 50,000-mile lifetime will be 0.00875. In effect, after 10,000 miles of use, the latter tire will assume the same wear and rolling resistance profiles as the former. Although its RRC starts out 10 percent higher, the latter tire's lifetime average RRC is only 6 percent higher. The thinner-tread tire will have lower average rolling resistance; however, it will also require replacement 20 percent sooner—not an attractive option from the perspective of consumer tire expenditures or controlling scrap tire populations.

These examples illustrate why reducing rolling resistance by designing tires with less tread depth would have both limited effects on fuel consumption and an undesirable response from motorists—and thus why such an approach would not likely be pursued generally. Indeed, because tire manufacturers must respond to consumer demand for wear resistance, they have sought alternative means of reducing rolling resistance with minimal loss of wear life. Some of these alternatives, including new tread materials, are discussed in the next scenario, along with approximations of their effects on consumer tire expenditures.

## Scenario 2: Reducing Rolling Resistance by Changing Tread Composition

Tire manufacturers and their materials suppliers have been actively seeking optimal means of reducing rolling resistance without sacrificing wear life and other aspects of performance. Unfortunately, the study committee is not aware of the various technologies—some proprietary—that have been developed and tried.

However, the important effect on rolling resistance of the tread compound and its constituent rubbers and reinforcing fillers is well established in the literature. Rubbers typically account for between 40 and 50 percent of tread volume and weight, and fillers typically account for 30 to 40 percent (Derham et al. 1988; Bethea et al. 1994; Russell 1993; Gent 2005, 30). Oils and other additives, which are used in processing and as material extenders, account for the rest of the volume and weight.

The tread's wear resistance, traction, and rolling resistance are determined in large part by the properties of these polymers and fillers, as well as by their concentrations, dispersion, and adhesion characteristics (Böhm et al. 1995; Wang et al. 2002). Consequently, fillers and polymers, as well as methods for mixing and curing them in the tread compound, have been primary targets of research and development aimed at reducing rolling resistance while preserving acceptable levels of other aspects of tire performance.

As discussed earlier, the predominant filler used in the tread compound is carbon black. A great deal of research has been devoted to modifying carbon black as a means of reducing rolling resistance. Among the approaches investigated have been varying its agglomerated particle size, manipulating its surface structure, and improving its dispersion through reactive mixing and other means (Russell 1993; McNeish and Byers 1997; Wang et al. 2002; Cook 2004). Because the supply of carbon black is a highly competitive business, materials suppliers have devoted much research and development to improving and distinguishing their products with regard to the effects on rolling resistance and other properties.

Silica is the next most common reinforcing filler in the tread compound. Silica has been added to tire rubber for decades, usually in combination with carbon black, largely because it improves cutting and chipping resistance of a tire as well as traction on snow and ice (Derham et al. 1988). However, silica does not develop a natural strong bond with rubber, owing to their different polarities. Silica tends to cluster rather than disperse evenly in the tread compound. This clustering not only makes processing more difficult, it increases the tread's hysteresis and results in poor wear. In the early 1990s, researchers found that applying organosilane coupling agents to silica during mixing resulted in more uniform filler dispersion and a consequent reduction in rolling resistance. In such applications to achieve lower rolling resistance, the silica–silane usually replaces a portion— seldom more than one-third—of the carbon black in the tread compound. Since this discovery, silica–silane systems have been promoted as a means of reducing rolling resistance without a severe penalty on traction or tread wear.

Replacing or modifying the filler is not the only means of reducing rolling resistance through changes in tread composition. Tread composition can be altered in other ways—for example, through changes in the rubbers, other tread components (e.g., oils, sulfur, zinc), and mixing processes. Examples of such modifications include the use of functionalized polymers that foster more uniform filler dispersion. Hydrogenated and tin-modified polymers have been used to reduce the rolling resistance of tires that are in production (Bethea et al. 1994; McNeish and Byers 1997). Of course, a more comprehensive approach to reducing rolling resistance would involve not only modifications of the tread compound but also changes in tire geometry and mass, belt and subtread materials, and the design and construction of other tire components such as the sidewall and casing.

The study committee could not examine all possible means of reducing rolling resistance—even means involving only changes in tread composition. Accordingly, the following estimates focus on the added material-related costs associated with a single change in tread composition: the partial substitution of silica–silane for carbon black. This scenario—admittedly simplified—provides an order-of-magnitude estimate of the effects on tire production costs that would be passed along to consumers in the prices paid for replacement tires possessing lower rolling resistance.

Market prices for carbon black and silica vary with supply and demand factors, including energy and transportation costs (Crump 2000). The prices paid by tire manufacturers for these materials are usually negotiated with suppliers and are not publicly available. While price differences between carbon black and silica vary at any given time and among suppliers, silica prices tend to be higher than carbon black prices by about one-third. Reference prices are $45 per 100 pounds of carbon black and $60 per 100 pounds of silica. About 5 pounds of silane, which costs about $3 per pound, is used for every 100 pounds of silica. Hence, the silica–silane combination costs about $75 per 100 pounds, compared with $45 for 100 pounds of carbon black. When silica–silane is used to reinforce tread stock, it seldom replaces more than one-third of the carbon black by volume or weight.

For an average passenger tire weighing 26.6 pounds,[9] the full tread band accounts for about 25 percent of the weight, or 6.7 pounds. Most of this tread weight is from the polymers as well as oils and other additives used in the tread compound. If it is assumed that reinforcing filler accounts for

---

[9] The average weight of tires in the RMA data set is 26.6 pounds.

35 percent of the tread's weight, the filler's total weight is about 2.3 pounds. If carbon black is used exclusively as the filler, its material costs will be $1.04 per tire ($0.45 per pound × 2.3 pounds). Replacing one-third (or 0.76 pound) of the 2.3 pounds of carbon black with an equal weight of silica–silane will raise the cost of filler material to about $1.26 per tire ($0.45 per pound × 1.54 pounds + $0.75 per pound × 0.76 pound), an increase in filler costs of $0.22 per tire.

Of course, estimates of raw material costs will not capture all manufacturing costs associated with substituting silica–silane for carbon black. The processing of silica–silane differs from that of carbon black. The former usually requires reactive mixing to raise the mixing temperature sufficiently to allow silica and silane to bond. The addition of silane also lengthens the curing time required for tread compounds and produces emissions of ethanol, which is a reactive compound subject to federal and state air quality controls (Joshi 2005). There are reports that silica, which is harder and contains more water than carbon black, can accelerate the wear of mixing devices from abrasion and corrosion (Borzenski 2004). While the added processing time, emissions mitigation, and equipment maintenance may not require large-scale plant investments, they will introduce additional production costs beyond the tread material expenses alone. It is reasonable to assume that these other costs would be at least as large as the silica–silane material expense, which would add another $0.22 to tire production costs and bring the total to $0.44 per tire.

The purpose of these calculations is not to develop a precise estimate of added costs but to get a sense of their scale and potential to translate into higher tire prices. Only the tire manufacturers can offer precise estimates of the effects on production costs and pricing, which are proprietary in nature and will depend in part on fluctuations in material costs and the pricing and cost allocation procedures of individual manufacturers. The estimates, though rough, suggest that the added cost of silica–silane will be less than $0.50 per tire. To be even more cautious, however, the committee assumes a resultant increase of $1 in the retail price of the tire. This added margin factors in the uncertainties noted above with regard to effects on tire manufacturing processes (e.g., emissions mitigation, equipment maintenance) as well as any cost markups that are successfully passed along to consumers. For an average tire priced at $97, a $1 price increase represents a premium of slightly more than 1 percent and would cause consumer tire expenditures to rise by an average of $1.14 per year assuming that tire wear life remains unchanged (since, on average, 1.14 replacement tires are purchased by motorists each year). For the 175 million passenger vehicles equipped with replacement tires, the total expenditure would be about $200 million per year (175 million × $1.14).

The application of silica–silane would likely be accompanied by other changes in tire materials and designs to achieve lower rolling resistance. Therefore, it is not possible to state with certainty that consumers would only pay about $1 more per tire in practice or that the tires would be comparable in all respects—including wear resistance, traction capability, and other properties—with tires having higher rolling resistance. The calculations do suggest that additional tire production costs are likely to result in a modest, rather than a dramatic, change in tire prices.

Unquestionably, an important consideration for consumers is tire wear life. While silica–silane systems are promoted as having wear and traction characteristics comparable with those of conventional tread compounds, the committee cannot verify these claims. Even a relatively small reduction in average wear life, on the order of a few percentage points, would result in corresponding increases in tire purchases and scrap tires. The estimates presented earlier in this chapter suggest that each 1 percent reduction in tire life would cost motorists an average of about $1.20 more per year in tire-related expenditures. Hence, if average tire life is shortened by as little as 5 percent, all or a significant portion of the annual fuel savings associated with lower rolling resistance would be offset.

## OVERALL EFFECT ON CONSUMER EXPENDITURES

The time that might be required to achieve a 10 percent reduction in the average rolling resistance of replacement tires is not considered here because it would depend on the specific means of achieving the reduction. At a minimum, such a reduction would likely require at least as many years as required to turn over most of the tires in the fleet. If new technologies were introduced to bring about the reduction, an unspecified amount of time for product development and market penetration would be required. As calculated above, such a reduction in average rolling resistance would save motorists an average of $12 to $24 per year in fuel expenditures, or $1.20 to $2.40 for every 1 percent reduction in the average rolling resistance experienced by replacement tires used on passenger vehicles.

Estimating the effect of reducing rolling resistance on tire expenditures is further complicated because of the numerous ways by which rolling resistance can be reduced. To gauge these costs, two scenarios were presented. One assumes that informed consumers would purchase more tires with lower rolling resistance from the selection of replacement tires already on the market. This is a conceivable scenario because today's replacement tires already exhibit much variation in rolling resistance, even among tires that are comparable in size and various performance ratings. Data available on replacement tires do not show a clear pattern of price differentials among replacement tires that vary in rolling resistance. This suggests that such a shift in consumer purchases would not be accompanied by higher average tire prices and tire expenditures as long as wear resistance does not suffer.

A possible concern is that consumers, demanding fuel economy, would purchase more tires with shorter wear life in the event that reducing tread thickness is the primary means employed by tire manufacturers to achieve lower rolling resistance. The estimates developed here suggest that each 1 percent reduction in tire wear life will cost consumers about $1.20 per year in additional tire expenditures. A shift in purchases that favors tires with shorter wear life could therefore result in higher tire expenditures that offset fuel savings. However, this outcome is unlikely as a practical matter. Not only would the fuel savings from this approach be small, but consumers would quickly observe and seek to avoid the trade-off, given their long-demonstrated interest in prolonging tire wear life. Indeed, reducing tread depth does not appear to be the only, or the most common, method for achieving lower rolling resistance among tires already on the market.

Tire manufacturers and their suppliers have been actively researching new materials and technologies to reduce rolling resistance without compromising wear resistance and traction. These materials and technologies tend to be more costly than are those used in conventional tires. Rough estimates of the additional cost of modifying tread composition to reduce rolling resistance suggest a price premium that is on the order of $1 per tire.

In practice, changes in tread composition to reduce rolling resistance tend to be made as part of more comprehensive changes in tire design, construction, and dimensions. The committee could not find comprehensive quantitative information on how such changes, taken together, would affect tire prices and other aspects of tire performance such as traction and wear resistance.

## REFERENCES

*Abbreviations*

EIA     Energy Information Administration
RMA     Rubber Manufacturers Association

Bethea, T. W., W. L. Hergenrother, F. J. Clark, and S. S. Sarker. 1994. Techniques to Reduce Tread Hysteresis. *Rubber and Plastics News,* Aug. 29.

Böhm, G. A., M. N. Nguyen, and W. M. Cole. 1995. Flocculation of Carbon Black in Filled Rubber Compounds. Presented to the Society of Rubber Industry, International Rubber Conference, Kobe, Japan.

Borzenski, F. J. 2004. Internal Wear of the Batch Mixer. Presented at International Tire Exhibition and Conference, Akron, Ohio, Sept. 21–23.

Cook, S. 2004. Low Rolling Resistance and Good Wet Grip with Silica. *Tire Technology International 2004.*

Crump, E. L. 2000. *Economic Impact Analysis for the Proposed Carbon Black Manufacturing NESHAP.* Report EPA-452/D-00-003. Office of Air Quality Planning Standards, U.S. Environmental Protection Agency, May.

Derham, C. J., R. Newell, and P. M. Swift. 1988. The Use of Silica for Improving Tread Grip in Winter Tyres. *NR Technology,* Vol. 19, No. 1, pp. 1–9.

EIA. 2005. *Annual Energy Outlook 2006* (early website release). U.S. Department of Energy, Washington, D.C.

Gent, A. N. 2005. Mechanical Properties of Rubber. In *The Pneumatic Tire* (J. D. Walter and A. N. Gent, eds.), National Highway Traffic Safety Administration, Washington, D.C., pp. 28–79.

Joshi, P. G. 2005. Low-VOC Silanes. *Tire Technology International 2005,* pp. 126–129.

McNeish, A., and J. Byers. 1997. Low Rolling Resistance Tread Compounds: Some Compounding Solutions. Presentation to Rubber Division, American Chemical Society, May 6, Anaheim, Calif.

Modern Tire Dealer. 2006. *Modern Tire Dealer's Facts Issue.* www.moderntiredealer.com. Jan.

RMA. 2005. *Factbook 2005: U.S. Tire Shipment Activity Report for Statistical Year 2004.* Washington, D.C.

Russell, R. M. 1993. Compounding for Wet Grip. *Tire Technology International 1993,* pp. 14–19.

Small, K., and K. Van Dender. 2005. *Fuel Efficiency and Motor Vehicle Travel: The Declining Rebound Effect.* Economic Working Paper 05-06-03 (revised December). University of California at Irvine.

Wang, M. J., Y. Kutsovsky, P. Zhang, G. Mehos, L. J. Murphy, and K. Mahmud. 2002. *KGK Kautschuk Gummi Kunststoffe 55.*

# 6

# Findings, Conclusions, and Recommendations

The technical literature and empirical evidence have been reviewed in this study to gain a better understanding of how the rolling resistance characteristics of tires relate to vehicle fuel economy, tire wear life, traction, and other aspects of tire performance. The focus has been on passenger tires sold for replacement, although it is recognized that original equipment (OE) tires lead many of the design trends and technologies emerging in the replacement market. The study has revealed variability in rolling resistance characteristics among replacement tires. Rolling resistance not only differs among tires when they are new but also changes as tires are used and maintained. The findings in this study make it possible to approximate the effect of a plausible reduction in the average rolling resistance of replacement tires in the passenger vehicle fleet on vehicle fuel economy. They also permit estimation of possible effects on tire wear life and operating performance of means of reducing rolling resistance.

Key study findings and estimates are consolidated to begin the chapter. They provide the basis for a series of conclusions in response to the specific questions asked by Congress. Taken together, the findings and conclusions persuade the committee that consumers will benefit from having greater access to information on the influence of passenger tires on vehicle fuel economy. They will also benefit from complementary information stressing the importance of proper tire inflation and maintenance to fuel economy, safe operation, and prolonged wear. Hence, the committee recommends that the National Highway Traffic Safety Administration (NHTSA) begin gathering this information and communicating it to the public, in close cooperation with the tire industry.

## KEY FINDINGS AND ESTIMATES

### Rolling resistance has a meaningful effect on vehicle fuel consumption.

For conventional passenger vehicles, most of the energy contained in a gallon of motor fuel is lost as heat during engine combustion and from friction in the driveline, axles, and wheel assemblies. Some of the energy produced by the engine is consumed during idling and by vehicle accessories. Only about 12 to 20 percent of the energy originating in the fuel tank is ultimately transmitted to the wheels as mechanical energy to propel the vehicle. Rolling resistance consumes about one-third of this transmitted energy.

In one sense, rolling resistance consumes only a small fraction of the total energy extracted from a gallon of fuel. In another sense, a reduction in rolling resistance will reduce demand for mechanical energy at the axles. This will have a multiplier effect because it will translate into fewer gallons of fuel being pumped to the engine in the first place.

The overall effect of a reduction in rolling resistance on vehicle fuel economy will depend on a number of factors, including the underlying efficiency of the engine and driveline as well as the relative amounts of energy consumed by other factors, such as aerodynamic drag and vehicle accessories. For most passenger vehicles, a 10 percent reduction in rolling resistance will have the practical effect of improving vehicle fuel economy by about 1 to 2 percent.

### Tires are the main source of rolling resistance.

The rolling resistance encountered by a vehicle can be extreme when it is driven on a soft or rough surface, such as a gravel or dirt road. On hard paved surfaces, which are more common for the operation of passenger vehicles, the main source of rolling resistance is the repeated flexing of the vehicle's tires as they roll. Through an effect known as hysteresis, this repeated flexing causes mechanical energy to be converted to heat. More mechanical energy must be supplied by the engine to replace the energy lost as heat from hysteresis. The design, construction, and materials of tires, as well as their maintenance, their condition, and operating conditions, affect the rate of energy loss. For most normal driving, a tire's rolling resistance characteristics will not change in response to an increase or decrease in vehicle travel speed.

**Tires differ in their rolling resistance.**

All tires cause rolling resistance, but to differing degrees. To improve traction and prolong wear, the tread component of the tire must have a substantial portion of the deformable, hysteretic material in the tire. The type and amount of material in the tread are therefore important determinants of rolling resistance. Other tire features and design parameters affect rolling resistance as well, including tire mass, geometry, and construction type.

About 80 percent, or 200 million, of the 250 million passenger tires shipped each year in the United States go to the replacement market, while the remaining 50 million are installed on new passenger vehicles as original equipment. There is considerable evidence to suggest that OE tires cause less rolling resistance, on average, than do replacement tires. Automobile manufacturers specify the tires installed on each of their vehicles; they tailor tire properties and designs to each vehicle's appearance, suspension, steering, and braking systems. Rolling resistance is usually one of the specified properties since it can affect a vehicle's ability to meet federal standards for fuel economy. Replacement tires, in contrast, are typically designed by tire manufacturers in a more general fashion to suit a wide range of in-use vehicles and a more diverse set of user requirements. The emphasis placed on characteristics such as traction, wear resistance, and rolling resistance can vary widely from tire to tire, depending on the demands of the specific segment of the replacement market.

Individual tires that start out with different rolling resistance—whether OE or replacement tires—will not retain the same differential over their service lives. Rolling resistance generally diminishes with tire use, and differences among tires will change. The many physical changes that tires undergo as they are used and age will modify rolling resistance over their life span. In particular, the loss of hysteretic tread material due to wear causes rolling resistance to decline. The rolling resistance of a properly inflated tire will typically decline by more than 20 percent over its service life.

**Tire condition and maintenance have important effects on rolling resistance.**

How well tires are maintained has a critical effect on their rolling resistance. Proper tire inflation is especially important in controlling rolling resistance because tires deform more when they are low on air. For typical passenger tires inflated to pressures of 24 to 36 pounds per square inch (psi), each 1-psi drop in inflation pressure will increase rolling resistance by about 1.4 percent. Hence, a drop in pressure from 32 to 24 psi—a significant degree of underinflation that would not be apparent by casually viewing the shape of the tire—increases a tire's rolling resistance by more than 10 percent. At pressures below 24 psi, rolling resistance increases even more rapidly with declining inflation pressure. Tire misalignment and misbalancing are among other installation and maintenance factors that increase vehicle energy consumption from rolling resistance as well as other drag forces.

### Tire rolling resistance characteristics can be measured and compared.

By holding inflation pressure and other operating conditions constant, a tire's rolling resistance characteristic can be measured for the purposes of design specification and comparisons with other tires. A tire's rolling resistance characteristic is normally expressed as a rate, or coefficient, with respect to the wheel load (that is, the weight on each wheel). A tire's rolling resistance increases in proportion to the wheel load.

The large majority of new passenger tires, properly inflated, have rolling resistance coefficients ranging from 0.007 to 0.014, with most having values closer to the average of about 0.01. Thus, the rolling resistance experienced by a passenger vehicle weighing 4,000 pounds with new tires may range from 28 to 56 pounds, or 7 to 14 pounds per tire. All else remaining constant, a vehicle equipped with a set of passenger tires having an average rolling resistance coefficient of 0.01 will consume about 1 to 2 percent less fuel than will a vehicle with tires having a coefficient of 0.011. Whether such a differential in fuel economy would be observed at all points in the lifetime of the two sets of tires will depend in large part on how their respective rolling resistance characteristics change with tire condition and tread wear.

### Progress has been made in reducing tire rolling resistance.

Significant progress has been made in reducing passenger tire rolling resistance during the past three decades through changes in tire designs, construction, and materials. The mass introduction of radial tires in the 1970s caused rolling resistance in new passenger tires to decline by about 25 percent. Subsequent changes in tire designs and materials have led to further reductions. Comparisons of the rolling resistance values of samples of new replacement radial tires sold today with those of radial tires sold 25 years ago show this progress. The lowest rolling resistance values measured in today's new tires are 20 to 30 percent lower than the lowest values measured among replacement tires sampled during the early 1980s.

However, the spread in rolling resistance values has increased over time, which is attributable to a proliferation in tire sizes, types, and speed capabilities. The average rolling resistance measured for new tires has therefore not changed as dramatically: it has declined by about 10 percent during the past decade. For reasons related to their design and construction requirements, tires with high speed ratings tend to have higher-than-average rolling resistance. These tires have become more popular in the replacement market.

Rolling resistance is not governed by a single set of tire design and construction variables. Even when tires are grouped by common size and speed ratings, the difference in rolling resistance values among tires often exceeds 20 percent. The data suggest that many design and construction variables can be adjusted to influence rolling resistance.

**Tires with lower rolling resistance and generally accepted traction capability are now on the market.**

Tire rolling resistance and traction characteristics are related because they are both heavily influenced by the tire's tread. The main function of the tread is traction, with thicker and deeper-grooved treads generally having better traction on wet, snowy, or otherwise contaminated road surfaces. Although a large amount of hysteretic material in the tread is usually advantageous for such traction capability, it can be a primary source of rolling resistance.

Passenger tires are rated for wet traction capability as part of the federal government's Uniform Tire Quality Grading (UTQG) system. Data available to the committee on replacement tires indicate that tires with the highest UTQG traction grade (AA) typically have high speed ratings and are often marketed as very-high-performance tires. Such tires seldom exhibit lower-than-average rolling resistance. This relationship should be expected, since wet traction and responsive stopping capability are fundamental to the design and construction of very-high-performance tires.

The large majority of tires in the marketplace, however, are designed to achieve the more modest UTQG system grade of A for traction. Among these tires, there is a much wider spread in rolling resistance values, and many such tires exhibit lower-than-average rolling resistance. Differences of 10 percent or more in rolling resistance are common among these tires, which suggests the technical feasibility and practicality of lowering rolling resistance while maintaining generally accepted levels of traction capability.

**The relationship between tire rolling resistance and wear resistance depends on many tire design variables.**

Tread wear is the main determinant of tire life. Shorter tire wear life results in more scrap tires and in consumers spending more on tire replacement, both of which are undesirable. Consequently, tire companies and their material suppliers have invested in research and development to find ways to reduce rolling resistance with minimal adverse effects on tread wear. The relationship between rolling resistance and wear resistance has been found to be determined by a combination of factors, including the type and amount of materials in the tread and the tread's design and dimensions.

Numerous changes in tread materials and formulations, including modifications of polymers and carbon black fillers and the substitution of silica–silane fillers, have been examined with the intent of reducing rolling resistance with few adverse side effects. Because many of these systems are proprietary, their cost, levels of use, and effect on tread wear are not well documented. However, it is clear from observing OE tires, and their acceptance by automobile manufacturers, that much progress has been made over the past two decades in the development of technologies and systems to reduce rolling resistance. Further advances in OE tires are anticipated and are likely to flow into the replacement market.

Another apparent way to reduce rolling resistance is to build tires with less tread material. This could have adverse effects on wear life and traction. In practice, tire designers can reduce tread mass and volume through combinations of changes in tread depth, width, shoulder profile, and section width. Data comparing rolling resistance and the single dimension of tread depth (the tread dimension that is most commonly listed for passenger tires) were examined in this study. They show that rolling resistance coefficients measured for new tires decline as tread depth declines. The data suggest that reducing new-tire tread depth by 2/32 inch, or almost 20 percent for the average tire in the study data set, will reduce new-tire rolling resistance coefficients by close to 10 percent. However, each reduction in tread depth of 1/32 inch is associated with lower UTQG tread wear ratings—about 5 percent lower on average. As might be expected, thinner tread is associated with shorter wear life, if compensating effects that may be achieved by altering materials and other tire design and construction technologies are disregarded.

Compared with an otherwise equivalent tire starting out with thicker tread, a tire starting out with thinner tread will yield fuel savings for a limited period. These savings will occur only during those miles traveled while the thicker-treaded tire is wearing down to the initial depth of the thinner-treaded tire. When the added tread thickness is gone, the two tires will essentially assume the same wear and rolling resistance profile per mile. The thinner-treaded tire will wear out sooner. Over its life, the tire starting out with less tread will exhibit slightly lower average rolling resistance per mile, but it will require earlier replacement at a cost to the motorist and lead to an increase in scrap tires.

### Reducing rolling resistance saves fuel.

If the average rolling resistance exhibited by replacement tires in the passenger vehicle fleet were to be reduced by 10 percent, motorists would save $12 to $24 per year in fuel expenses, or roughly $1.20 to $2.40 for every 1 percent reduction in average rolling resistance. This assumes a long-term average price of $2 per gallon for gasoline and diesel fuel, as recently projected by the U.S. Department of Energy. The time required to achieve a 10 percent reduction in the average rolling resistance of replacement tires is not considered here but would depend on how the reduction is brought about. Presumably, it would require at least as many years as needed to turn over most passenger tires in the fleet, and perhaps added time for the development and introduction of any required technologies.

Extrapolation to the 175 million passenger vehicles using replacement tires results in an estimate of national fuel savings ranging from $2 billion to $4 billion per year.

### Reducing rolling resistance will have modest effects on tire expenditures.

The effect of reducing rolling resistance on consumer tire expenditures is difficult to estimate without knowing the precise magnitude of the reduction or how it would occur. A 10 percent reduction in the average rolling resistance of replacement tires on the road could occur through a combination of changes in the distribution of tires purchased and greater use being made of various technologies to reduce rolling resistance. It could also be achieved in part through more vigilant tire maintenance. Different approaches to achieving a reduction must be considered when effects on tire expenditures are estimated.

Data on new replacement tires do not show any clear pattern of price differences among tires that vary in rolling resistance but that are comparable in many other respects such as traction, size, and speed rating. This result suggests that consumers buying existing tires with lower rolling resistance will not necessarily pay more for these tires or incur higher tire expenditures overall, as long as average tire wear life is not shortened. Calculations in this report suggest that each 1 percent reduction in tire wear life costs consumers about $1.20 more per year in added tire expenses because of more frequent tire replacement. Consequently, a shift in the kinds of tires purchased that has the effect of reducing average rolling resistance but also reducing the average life of replacement tires will cause higher tire expenditures, as well as larger numbers of scrap tires. A reduction in average tire life of as little as 5 percent could cause an increase in tire expenditures that offsets all or a large portion of the savings in fuel. Because of such poor economics, reductions in tread depth and other measures to reduce rolling resistance that have significant impacts on tire wear life could be unwise and may be unacceptable.

Tire manufacturers and their suppliers have been actively researching new materials and technologies to reduce rolling resistance that will affect wear resistance and traction only minimally. These materials and technologies, many focused on tread composition, tend to be more costly to apply. However, rough estimates suggest a small addition to tire production costs, on the order of $1 per tire. In practice, tread modifications designed to reduce rolling resistance tend to be applied as part of a broader array of changes in tire design, construction, and dimensions. The committee could not find detailed quantitative information on how such practical changes, in their many potential combinations, are likely to affect other aspects of tire performance such as traction and wear resistance.

Motorists currently purchase 200 million replacement tires per year. An increase in tire prices averaging $1 per tire would cost vehicle owners $200 million per year, if tire wear and replacement rates are held constant. Total national spending on replacement tires would thus increase in this instance by about $200 million per year. U.S. consumers have demonstrated a desire to maintain, and indeed extend, tire wear life, which suggests that poor wear performance would be unacceptable. If tire wear life were diminished on average, additional tire expenditures could greatly exceed $200 million per year, owing to the need for more frequent tire replacement.

If reductions in rolling resistance are achieved through more vigilant tire and inflation maintenance, tire wear life would be prolonged, and expenditures on tires by consumers would be reduced.

## CONCLUSIONS IN RESPONSE TO STUDY CHARGE

Congress called for this study of the feasibility and effects of lowering the rolling resistance of replacement tires installed on cars and light trucks used for passenger transportation. Although many gaps in information and understanding persist, the findings and estimates presented above are helpful in answering the series of questions asked. Specifically, Congress asked how lowering replacement tire rolling resistance would affect

- Motor fuel use;
- Tire wear life and the creation of scrap tires;
- Tire performance characteristics, including those relevant to vehicle safety; and
- Tire expenditures by consumers.

Drawing on the study findings, the committee offers its assessment of the feasibility of reducing rolling resistance and its conclusions in response to the individual elements of the study charge. The findings and conclusions, coupled with other insights gained during the course of the study, convince the committee that tire energy performance deserves greater attention from government, industry, and consumers. A recommendation for congressional action is offered in light of the following conclusions.

## Feasibility of Lowering Rolling Resistance in Replacement Tires

**Reducing the average rolling resistance of replacement tires by a magnitude of 10 percent is technically and economically feasible.** A tire's overall contribution to vehicle fuel consumption is determined by its rolling resistance averaged over its lifetime of use. A reduction in the average rolling resistance of replacement tires in the fleet can occur through various means. Consumers could purchase more tires that are now available with lower rolling resistance, tire designs could be modified, and new tire technologies that offer reduced rolling resistance could be introduced. More vigilant maintenance of tire inflation pressure will further this outcome. In the committee's view, there is much evidence to suggest that reducing the average rolling resistance of replacement tires by a magnitude of 10 percent is feasible and attainable within a decade through combinations of these means.

Rolling resistance varies widely among replacement tires already on the market, even among tires that are comparable in price, size, traction, speed capability, and wear resistance. Consumers, if sufficiently informed and interested, could bring about a reduction in average rolling resistance by adjusting their tire purchases and by taking proper care of their tires once in service, especially by maintaining recommended inflation pressure. The committee does not underestimate the challenge of changing consumer preferences and behavior. This could be a difficult undertaking, and it must begin with information concerning the tire's influence on fuel economy being made widely and readily available to tire buyers and sellers. A significant and sustained reduction in rolling resistance is difficult to imagine under any circumstances without informed and interested consumers.

The committee observes that consumers now have little, if any, practical way of assessing how tire choices can affect vehicle economy.

## Influence on Vehicle Fuel Economy

**Tires and their rolling resistance characteristics can have a meaning-ful effect on vehicle fuel economy and consumption.** A 10 percent re-duction in average rolling resistance, if achieved for the population of vehicles using replacement tires, promises a 1 to 2 percent increase in the fuel economy of these vehicles. About 80 percent of passenger cars and light trucks are equipped with replacement tires. Assuming that the number of miles traveled does not change, a 1 to 2 percent increase in the fuel economy of these vehicles would save about 1 billion to 2 billion gallons of fuel per year of the 130 billion gallons consumed by the entire passen-ger vehicle fleet. This fuel savings is equivalent to the fuel saved by taking 2 million to 4 million cars and light trucks off the road. In this context, a 1 to 2 percent reduction in the fuel consumed by passenger vehicles using replacement tires would be a meaningful accomplishment.

## Effects on Tire Wear Life and Scrap Tires

**The effects of reductions in rolling resistance on tire wear life and scrap tires are difficult to estimate because of the various ways by which rolling resistance can be reduced.** The tread is the main factor in tire wear life and the main component of the tire contributing to rolling resistance. Reductions in tread thickness, volume, and mass are among the means available to reduce rolling resistance, but they may be unde-sirable if they lead to shorter tire lives and larger numbers of scrap tires. Various tread-based technologies are being developed and used with the goal of reducing rolling resistance without significant effects on wear resistance. The practical effects of these technologies on tread wear and other tire performance characteristics have not been established quanti-tatively. However, continuing advances in tire technology hold much promise that rolling resistance can be reduced further without adverse effects on tire wear life and scrap tire populations.

## Effects on Traction and Safety Performance

**Although traction may be affected by modifying a tire's tread to reduce rolling resistance, the committee could not find safety consequences. Such consequences may be undetectable.** Changes are routinely made in tire designs, materials, and construction methods for reasons ranging from noise mitigation and ride comfort to steering response and styling. All can have implications for other tire properties and operating performance, including traction capability. Discerning the safety implications of small changes in tire traction characteristics associated with tread modifications to reduce rolling resistance may not be practical or even possible, especially since there is no single way to reduce rolling resistance. The committee could not find safety studies or vehicle crash data that provide insight into the safety impacts associated with large changes in traction capability, much less the smaller changes that may occur from modifying the tread to reduce rolling resistance.

### Effects on Consumer Fuel and Tire Expenditures

**Reducing the average rolling resistance of replacement tires promises fuel savings to consumers that exceed associated tire purchase costs, as long as tire wear life is not shortened.** A 10 percent reduction in rolling resistance can reduce consumer fuel expenditures by 1 to 2 percent for typical vehicles. This savings is equivalent to 6 to 12 gallons per year, or $12 to $24 if fuel is priced at $2 per gallon. Tire technologies available today to reduce rolling resistance would cause consumers to spend slightly more when they buy replacement tires, on the order of $1 to $2 per year. These technologies, however, may need to be accompanied by other changes in tire materials and designs to maintain the levels of wear resistance that consumers demand. While the effect of such accompanying changes on tire production costs and prices is unclear, the overall magnitude of the fuel savings suggests that consumers would likely incur net savings in their expenditures.

## RECOMMENDATIONS TO INFORM CONSUMERS

As a general principle, consumers benefit from the ready availability of easy-to-understand information on all major attributes of their purchases. Tires are no exception, and their influence on vehicle fuel economy is an attribute that is likely to be of interest to many tire buyers. Because tires are driven tens of thousands of miles, their influence on vehicle fuel consumption can extend over several years. Ideally, consumers would have access to information that reflects a tire's effect on fuel economy averaged over its anticipated lifetime of use, as opposed to a measurement taken during a single point in the tire's lifetime, usually when it is new. No standard measure of lifetime energy consumption is currently available, and the development of one deserves consideration. Until such a practical measure is developed, rolling resistance measurements of new tires can be informative to consumers, especially if they are accompanied by reliable information on other tire characteristics such as wear resistance and traction.

Advice on specific procedures for measuring and rating the influence of individual passenger tires on fuel economy and methods of conveying this information to consumers is outside the scope of this study. Nevertheless, the committee is persuaded that there is a public interest in consumers having access to such information. The public interest is comparable with that of consumers having information on tire traction and tread wear characteristics, which is now provided by industry as required by the federal Uniform Tire Quality Grading standards.

It is apparent that industry cooperation is essential in gathering and conveying tire performance information that consumers can use in making tire purchases. It is in the spirit of prompting and ensuring more widespread industry cooperation in the supply of useful and trusted purchase information that the committee makes the following recommendations.

**Congress should authorize and make sufficient resources available to NHTSA to allow it to gather and report information on the influence of individual passenger tires on vehicle fuel consumption. Information that best indicates a tire's contribution to vehicle fuel consumption and that can be effectively gathered, reported, and communicated to consumers buying tires should be sought. The effort should cover a large portion of the passenger tires sold in the United States and be comprehensive with regard to popular tire sizes, models, and types, both imported and domestic.**

**NHTSA should consult with the U.S. Environmental Protection Agency on means of conveying the information and ensure that the information is made widely available in a timely manner and is easily understood by both buyers and sellers. In the gathering and**

communication of this information, the agency should seek the active participation of the entire tire industry.

The effectiveness of this consumer information and the methods used for communicating it should be reviewed regularly. The information and communication methods should be revised as necessary to improve effectiveness. Congress should require periodic assessments of the initiative's utility to consumers, the level of cooperation by industry, and the resultant contribution to national goals pertaining to energy consumption.

Finally, even as motorists are advised of the energy performance of tires, they must appreciate that all tires require proper inflation and maintenance to achieve their intended levels of energy, safety, wear, and operating performance. As new technologies such as tire pressure monitoring systems, more energy-efficient tire designs, and run-flat constructions are introduced on a wider basis, they must have the effect of prompting more vigilant tire maintenance rather than fostering more complacency in this regard. Motorists must be alerted to the fact that even small losses in inflation pressure can greatly reduce tire life, fuel economy, safety, and operating performance. A strong message urging vigilant maintenance of inflation must therefore be a central part of communicating information on the energy performance of tires to motorists.

# Explanation and Comparison of Society of Automotive Engineers Test Procedures for Rolling Resistance

Marion G. Pottinger
*M'gineering, LLC*

Two standardized tests are used in the United States to measure the rolling resistance of tires. The two tests are detailed in recommended practices of the Society of Automotive Engineers (SAE): J1269, "Rolling Resistance Measurement Procedure for Passenger Car, Light Truck, and Highway Truck and Bus Tires,"[1] and J2452, "Stepwise Coastdown Methodology for Measuring Tire Rolling Resistance." J1269 is the older of the two practices. It was approved in 1979 and reaffirmed in 2000. J1269 is intended to "provide a way of gathering data on a uniform basis, to be used for various purposes (for example, tire comparisons, determination of load and pressure effects, correlation with test results from fuel consumption tests, etc.)."[2] J2452 was approved by SAE in 1999. Its primary intent is "estimation of the tire rolling resistance contribution to vehicle force applicable to SAE Vehicle Coastdown recommended practices J2263 and J2264."[3]

## COMMON FEATURES OF THE TWO TEST PRACTICES

The two practices have common features such as test wheel diameter, surface texture, and ambient temperature. The commonalities are noted in

---

[1] J1269 is accompanied by an information report, J1270, "Measurement of Passenger Car, Light Truck, and Highway Truck and Bus Tire Rolling Resistance."

[2] The quotation is drawn from the J1269 document.

[3] The quotation is drawn from the J2452 document.

**TABLE A-1**  Items Common to J1269 and J2452

| Item | Specification |
|---|---|
| Test wheel diameter | 1.7 m (67 in.) |
| Measurement methods[a] | Force |
| | Torque |
| Surface | 80-grit paper[b] |
| Allowed ambient temperature | 20°C (68°F) ≤ T ≤ 28°C (82°F) |
| Reference temperature | 24°C (75°F) |

[a] J1269 also allows rolling resistance determination by measurement of electrical power consumption, but this method is no longer in common use.
[b] This is actually an emery cloth. J2452 contains a surface conditioning procedure for the material.

Table A-1. The practices use the same test rims. The normally used test rims are the measuring rims,[4] but other rims approved in a tire and rim standards organization yearbook such as that of the Tire and Rim Association may be used. The rim used is always noted in the test report because rim width affects test results.

## DIFFERENCES BETWEEN THE TWO PRACTICES

There are a number of differences between the two practices, which are detailed below.

### Inflation Pressure and Load

Tire rolling resistance is dependent on inflation pressure and load. In both test practices inflation pressure is defined in terms of a base pressure. Base pressure is not defined in precisely the same manner in the two practices. In J1269 it is the inflation pressure molded on the tire sidewall together with the maximum load. This is straightforward for P-tires, but it only applies to single-tire loading in the case of LT-tires.[5] In J2452, P-tire base pressures are defined in the first table in the recommended practice.

---

[4] The design/measuring rim is the specific rim assigned to each specific tire designation to determine basic tire dimensions. This rim is specified for each tire designation in the yearbooks of tire and rim standards organizations such as the Tire and Rim Association, Inc.
[5] P-tires are passenger tires. LT-tires are light truck tires.

They are different from those given in J1269 for some tires. The base pressure for LT-tires matches that given in J1269.

In both practices load is defined in terms of maximum load. "Maximum load" is defined in both practices as the maximum load molded on the tire sidewall and listed as the load limit in the tire load tables of the current yearbook for the relevant tire and rim standards organization. For LT-tires this is the maximum load for single-tire operation.

## Test Elements

Test elements include break-in, warm-up, and the actual test conditions. Break-in is to be used with tires that change in dimensions or material properties during first operation. Break-in is usually not required since the first 30 minutes of warm-up for Test Condition 1 is considered to be an allowable substitute for formal break-in. Also, until the tire has passed through first operation, there is no way to determine whether it will change in dimensions or material properties. Furthermore, since the load and inflation for Test Condition 1 in J1269 and J2452 are not the same, the resultant effective break-in is Recommended Practice–specific.

During the warm-up process, which occurs before each test condition, the tire is brought to thermal equilibrium. There are two approved ways to perform the warm-up: timed and rolling resistance force rate of change determined. In the timed method the tire is operated for a defined time at the conditions for each test step before data acquisition for that step. For P-tires the time period before Condition 1 is 30 minutes. It is 10 minutes before other steps. For LT-tires the period before Condition 1 is 60 minutes. It is 15 minutes before other steps. In the rate of change method, after a short waiting period for Condition 1 (10 minutes for P-tires and 20 minutes for LT-tires) and without a waiting period for other conditions, the rolling resistance is monitored with equilibrium being defined to exist when the rolling resistance gradient is less than or equal to 0.13 newtons per minute over a 90-second period. Regardless of the warm-up method, once equilibrium formally exists for each condition, data acquisition can begin.

The test conditions used for P-tires are defined in Table A-2, and those for LT-tires are defined in Table A-3. The test conditions for J1269 and J2452 are not identical. The exact procedure for executing the test under the test conditions is discussed under the subject of test execution.

**TABLE A-2** Regulated Pressure Test Conditions for P-Tires

| | J1269 | | J2452 | |
|---|---|---|---|---|
| Test Point | % Max Load | Base Pressure ± (kPa) | % Max Load | Base Pressure ± (kPa) |
| 1 | 90 | −30 | 30 | +10 |
| 2 | 90 | +70 | 60 | −40 |
| 3 | 50 | −30 | 90 | +60 |
| 4 | 50 | +70 | 90 | −40 |

NOTE: There is a version of the J1269 procedure in which Step 1 is conducted under capped conditions. In this case, the inflation pressure is established cold, the valve cap is put in place, and all increases in pressure are due to the rising tire temperature during the warm-up period.

# HANDLING OF DATA CORRECTIONS

Raw data taken during testing contain tares (offsets), parasitic losses such as bearing losses, force measurement crosstalk, and perhaps alignment errors. Additional data besides the basic data acquired according to the section on test execution are required to eliminate these errors. These correction data are used during data analysis.

The load cell output with the test tire and rim mounted but not loaded is acquired for each test condition to obtain tares. During analysis, these data are subtracted from the data taken for the test condition to which they pertain.

With the tire loaded just enough so that it will continue to rotate, force or torque data, whichever are relevant for the test machine being used,

**TABLE A-3** Regulated Pressure Test Conditions for LT-Tires

| | J1269 | | J2452 | |
|---|---|---|---|---|
| Test Point | % Max Load | % Base Pressure | % Max Load | % Base Pressure |
| 1 | 100 | 110 | 20 | 110 |
| 2 | 70 | 60 | 40 | 50 |
| 3 | 70 | 110 | 40 | 100 |
| 4 | 40 | 30 | 70 | 60 |
| 5 | 40 | 60 | 100 | 100 |
| 6 | 40 | 110 | | |

are acquired for each speed. These data contain the parasitic bearing losses and aerodynamic losses. During analysis, these data are subtracted from the data taken for the test condition to which they pertain.

Crosstalk occurs in all multidimensional force measurement machines. A matrix to remove this effect is derived during machine calibration. If errors exist because of machine load application alignment imperfections not fully compensated by the crosstalk matrix, the test must be run in both directions of rotation on force measurement rolling resistance test machines, and the results must be averaged.

## HOW THE TESTS ARE EXECUTED

### J1269

With the test machine operating at a steady 80 km/h, data are acquired according to the following sequence:

- Warm-up at $P_1$ and $F_{Z1}$.
- Acquire data at $P_1$ and $F_{Z1}$.
- Warm-up at $P_2$ and $F_{Z2}$.
- Acquire data at $P_2$ and $F_{Z2}$.
  $\vdots$
- Acquire data at $P_n$ and $F_{Zn}$ as prescribed in the relevant practice.

### J2452

For each test condition, the tire is warmed up at 80 km/h until steady-state rolling resistance is achieved. At that point the tire is quickly accelerated to 115 km/h and then subjected to a stepwise approximation to a 180-second coastdown to 15 km/h. The stepwise approximation contains six or more approximately equally spaced steps. Figure A-1 is an example of such a coastdown.

## COMMON DATA ANALYSIS

The first step is to apply the required data corrections. At that point the rolling resistance is computed. Next the data are adjusted to give the rolling resistance at 24°C (75°F) by using Equation 1.

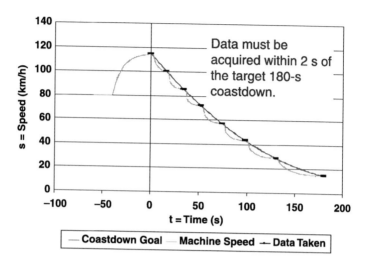

**FIGURE A-1** Example of stepwise coastdown in J2452 test practice.

$$RR_T = RR\left[1 + k\left(T_A - T_R\right)\right] \tag{1}$$

where

$RR_T$ = rolling resistance at 24°C,
$RR$ = rolling resistance at $T_A$,
$T_A$ = ambient temperature during a test condition, and
$T_R$ = reference temperature = 24°C.

The $k$-values given in J1269 and J2452 are not the same.

Since the data are taken on a 1.7-meter-diameter test dynamometer, they are not correct for other diameters, for example, ∞ (flat) or 1.22 meters (48 inches), which is used in federal vehicle emission and fuel economy tests. An approximate correction for curvature is obtained by applying the Clark equation, Equation 2.[6] Equation 3 is the Clark equation for the special case of a flat surface.

---

[6] The text of J2452 notes that the question of correction for curvature needs to be revisited; however, this has not been done since J2452 was adopted in 1999.

$$RR_2 = \{[(R_1/R_2)(R_2+r)]/(R_1+r)\}^{1/2}(RR_1) \tag{2}$$

$$RR_2 = [R_1/(R_1+r)]^{1/2}(RR_1) \tag{3}$$

where

$R_1$ = measurement surface radius,

$R_2$ = radius of the surface to which the data are being adjusted, and

$r$ = unloaded tire nominal radius.

## DATA FITTING

For modeling and other engineering purposes, empirical relationships are fit by using the J1269 and J2452 data. Because consistency with J1269 was not considered during the development of J2452, the J2452 equation does not devolve to the J1269 equation when velocity is set to 80 km/h. J1269 was not revised so that its equations are the J2452 equation at a single velocity.

For J1269 P-tire fitting,

$$RR_T = F_Z\left(A_0 + A_1 F_Z + A_2/P\right) \tag{4}$$

For J1269 LT-tire fitting,

$$RR_T = A_0 + A_1 F_Z + A_2/P + A_3 F_Z/P + A_4 F_Z/P^2 \tag{5}$$

In Equations 4 and 5, $F_Z$ is load, $P$ is inflation pressure, and $A_0, A_1, \ldots,$ $A_4$ are constants.

For J2452 fitting,

$$RR_T = P^\alpha F_Z^\beta\left(a + bV + cV^2\right) \tag{6}$$

where

$a, b, c, \alpha, \beta$ = constants;

$F_Z$ = load;

$P$ = inflation pressure; and

$V$ = speed.

## SINGLE-NUMBER EXPRESSION OF RESULTS

In comparing tire specifications, it is important to be able to character-
ize tire rolling resistance with a single number. The model derived from
J1269 or J2452 can be queried to yield a rolling resistance value at a single
point.

### Simplified Standard Reference Condition

Because of the possibility of needing to produce data on a large array of
tires, J2452 contains a Simplified Standard Reference Condition, which
yields data at the following single condition.

- Load = 70 percent of maximum,
- Inflation = base + 20 kPa, and
- $V = 80$ km/h.

(At the time this appendix was prepared, a single-point test at the Simplified Standard Reference Condition was in ballot as a revision of J1269.)

### Mean Equivalent Rolling Force

J2452 contains a method for deriving a single number representative of
a known driving cycle. This is the mean equivalent rolling force (MERF).
It is calculated by Equation 7.

$$\text{MERF} = \frac{\int_{t_0}^{t_f} RR \, dt}{\int_{t_0}^{t_f} dt} \tag{7}$$

where

> $RR$ = rolling resistance as a function of time within the chosen cycle,
> $t_f$ = final time in the cycle, and
> $t_0$ = initial time in the cycle.

Equation 7 is the time integration of the rolling resistance during the
cycle under study divided by the time during which the cycle occurs.

Typically, the cycle under consideration would be one of the federal test procedure (FTP) driving cycles such as the urban or highway schedule.

If MERF is computed for both FTP cycles, a MERF related to corporate average fuel economy (CAFE) can be computed as indicated in Equation 8.

$$MERF_{CAFE} = 0.55(MERF_{URBAN}) + 0.45(MERF_{HIGHWAY}) \qquad (8)$$

## Standard MERF

This is a MERF computed at the standard reference conditions discussed above.

# Study Committee
# Biographical Information

**Dale F. Stein,** *Chair,* is President Emeritus of Michigan Technological University. He has also been Vice President of Academic Affairs and Professor in the Departments of Metallurgical Engineering and Mining Engineering. He began his career as a Research Metallurgist at General Electric Research Laboratory. His major research interests are in the deformation and fracture of materials and the relationship between materials and the environment. Dr. Stein has an interest in the recycling and efficient use of materials. He was a pioneer in the application of auger spectroscopy to the solution of metallurgical problems and a leading authority on the mechanical properties of engineering materials. He is a Fellow of the Minerals, Metals and Materials Society; the American Society for Metals; and the American Association for the Advancement of Science. He has been a member of more than 20 committees and panels of the National Academies. He has chaired many of these committees, including the Committee on Novel Approaches to the Management of Greenhouse Gas Emissions from Energy Systems, the Committee on Materials Science and Engineering, and the Transportation Research Board's (TRB's) Research and Technology Coordinating Committee for the Federal Highway Administration. He was a member of the National Materials Advisory Board. Dr. Stein was elected to the National Academy of Engineering in 1986. He holds a BS in metallurgy from the University of Minnesota and a PhD in metallurgy from Rensselaer Polytechnic Institute.

**James E. Bernard** is Anson Marston Distinguished Professor of Engineering at Iowa State University and Director of the Virtual Reality Applications Center. His research interests include vehicle dynamics and driving simulation, and he is a member of the Vehicle Dynamics Subcommittee of the Society of Automotive Engineers (SAE). He has written numerous papers relating to motor vehicle rollover and associated vehicle test methods, including a comprehensive literature review. Dr. Bernard has received a number of awards for his contributions to graduate and undergraduate teaching, including the SAE Ralph R. Teetor Award for "significant contributions to teaching, research and student development." He has received awards for his technical research papers from *Tire Science and Technology* and the MSC.Nastran World Users Conference. He was a member of the National Academies Committee for the Motor Vehicle Rollover Rating System Study. He held teaching and research positions at the University of Michigan and Michigan State University before joining the faculty of Iowa State University as Professor and Chairman of Mechanical Engineering in 1983. He received his BS, MS, and PhD in engineering mechanics from the University of Michigan.

**John Eagleburger** retired in 2003 as Manager of Products Adjustments and Claims Performance for Goodyear Tire Company. From 1995 to 2002, he was Leader of the General Motors (GM) Team of the Akron Technical Center, where he managed a multidisciplinary engineering team in the design, testing, and approval of original equipment manufacturer passenger and light truck tires for GM vehicles. From 1988 to 1995, he was based in Tokyo as Goodyear's Manager of Engineering and supplied tire products to Japanese and Korean automobile makers. He was previously GM account manager for Goodyear based in Detroit and manager of technical coordination for tire standards. Mr. Eagleburger began his career at Goodyear in 1965, serving as a tire design engineer and project engineer. He was active in SAE and served on several technical committees during his career. He holds a BS in mechanical engineering from the University of Wisconsin.

**Richard J. Farris** is Distinguished University Professor Emeritus at the Silvio Conte National Center for Polymer Research in the Polymer Science and Engineering Department, University of Massachusetts, Amherst. His research interests are in experimental mechanics, high-performance fibers, rubber elasticity and thermodynamics, particulate composites, and recycling of elastomers. He has more than 300 refereed publications and 16 patents. Dr. Farris served as Chairman of the Gordon Research Conference on Composites and the Gordon Research

Conference on High-Performance Thermo-Setting Materials and as a member of numerous advisory committees for the National Aeronautics and Space Administration and other government agencies. He is a Fellow of the Society of Plastics Engineers and served as a member of the National Academies Panel on Structural and Multifunctional Materials. He is the recipient of the Roon Award of the Federation of Societies for Coating Technology (1998), the Malcolm Pruitt Award of the Council for Chemical Research (2003), the George Stafford Whitby Award from the Rubber Division of the American Chemical Society (2005), and the Founder's Award from the Society of Plastics Engineers (2006). He holds an MS and a PhD in civil engineering from the University of Utah.

**David Friedman** is Research Director for the Union of Concerned Scientists' (UCS) Clean Vehicles Program. He is the author or coauthor of more than 30 technical papers and reports on advances in conventional, fuel cell, and hybrid electric vehicles and alternative energy sources with an emphasis on clean and efficient technologies. Before joining UCS in 2001, he worked for the University of California at Davis (UC Davis) in the Fuel Cell Vehicle Modeling Program, where he developed simulation tools to evaluate fuel cell technology for automotive applications. He worked on the UC Davis FutureCar team to build a hybrid electric family car that doubled fuel economy. He previously worked at Arthur D. Little researching fuel cell, battery electric, and hybrid electric vehicle technologies, as well as photovoltaics. Mr. Friedman is a member of the Board on Energy and Environmental Systems' Panel on Prospective Benefits of the Department of Energy's Light-Duty Hybrid Vehicle R&D Program and previously served on that board's Panel on the Prospective Benefits of the Department of Energy's Fuel Cell R&D Program. He earned a bachelor's degree in mechanical engineering from Worcester Polytechnic Institute and is a doctoral candidate in transportation technology and policy at UC Davis.

**Patricia S. Hu** is Director of the Center for Transportation Analysis at the Engineering Science and Technology Division of Oak Ridge National Laboratory (ORNL). She has been at ORNL since 1982 and in her current position since 2000. At ORNL, she has led many projects in transportation statistics and analysis. She chairs TRB's Standing Committee on National Data Requirements and Programs and serves on other TRB standing committees. She served on the Editorial Advisory Board of the international journal *Accident Analysis and Prevention* from 1996 to 1998 and has served on the Editorial Advisory Board of the *Journal of Transportation Statistics* since 1998. She led a team supported by the Transportation Security Administration studying the domain awareness of U.S. food supply chains by linking and analyzing geospatial data on transportation networks, traffic volume, choke points, freight flow, and traffic routing. She holds a bachelors degree from the National Chengchi University, Taipei, Taiwan, and an MS in mathematics and statistics from the University of Guelph, Ontario, Canada.

**Wolfgang G. Knauss** is Theodore von Kármán Professor of Aeronautics and Applied Mechanics at the California Institute of Technology. His work has centered on understanding the mechanics of time-dependent fracture in polymeric materials. He has served on several national committees and delegations, including the National Committee on Theoretical and Applied Mechanics (as chair), the U.S. delegation to the International Union of Theoretical and Applied Mechanics General Assembly, the Army Panel on Air and Ground Vehicle Technology, and the Aerospace Scientific Advisory Committee. Dr. Knauss has received numerous awards during his academic career, including Woodrow Wilson Foundation Fellowship and National Aeronautics and Space Administration Fellowship. He is an Elected Fellow of the Institute for the Advancement of Engineering, the American Society of Mechanical Engineers (ASME), and the National Academy of Mechanics. He was elected to the National Academy of Engineering in 1998 for engineering work on time-dependent fracture of polymers at interfaces and under dynamic loading. He was awarded the Senior U.S. Scientist Award by the Alexander von Humboldt Foundation and the Murray Medal of the Society of Experimental Mechanics. He holds a BS, an MS, and a PhD from the California Institute of Technology.

**Christopher L. Magee** is Professor of the Practice, Mechanical Engineering, at the Massachusetts Institute of Technology (MIT). He is also Engineering Systems Director at MIT's multidisciplinary Center for Innovation in Product Development. Before joining MIT in 2002, he worked for the Ford Motor Company, beginning in the Scientific Research

Laboratory and progressing through a series of management positions to Executive Director of Programs and Advanced Engineering. In the latter position, he had responsibility for all major technically advanced areas in Ford's product development organization. During his career at Ford, he made major contributions to the understanding of the transformation, structure, and strength of ferrous materials. He developed lightweight materials for automobile manufacturing and pioneered experimental work on high-rate structural collapse to improve vehicle crashworthiness. He initiated Ford's computer-aided engineering for structural and occupant simulation for crashworthiness. Dr. Magee is internationally recognized for this work and received the Alfred Nobel Award of the American Society of Civil Engineers. He was elected to the National Academy of Engineering in 1996. He has served on several National Academies committees, including the Panel on Materials Research Opportunities and Needs in Materials Science and Engineering and the Panel on Theoretical Foundations for Decision Making in Engineering Design. He currently serves on the Committee on Review of the FreedomCAR and Fuel Research Program. He earned a BS and a PhD from Carnegie-Mellon University and an MBA from Michigan State University.

**Marion G. Pottinger** retired in 2003 as Technical Director, Smithers Scientific Services, Inc. He is now a private consultant. Smithers Scientific Services, where he worked for 15 years, is an independent testing, research, and consulting firm. Before joining Smithers, he was Associate Research and Development Fellow at Uniroyal Goodrich Tire Company, where he focused on the development of high-performance tires and instruments to measure tire wear. Before 1985, he was a senior manager in the BFGoodrich research and development unit, responsible for research in acoustics, vibration, vehicle dynamics, tire force and moment, wear, and structural mechanics. Dr. Pottinger has published more than 50 articles and book chapters on tires, gearing, high-performance composites, and instruments. He is President Emeritus of the Tire Society and a member of SAE's Highway Tire Forum Committee, Vehicle Dynamics Standards Committee, and Chassis and Suspension Committee. He is a member of the ASTM F-09 Committee on Tires. He holds a BS in mechanical engineering from the University of Cincinnati and an MS and a PhD in mechanical engineering from Purdue University.

**Karl J. Springer** is retired Vice President of Automotive Products and Emissions Research at Southwest Research Institute. He oversaw a staff of more than 600 employees engaged in research, testing, and evaluation of diesel and gasoline engine lubricants, fuels, fluids, emissions, and components for automotive, truck, bus, and tractor products. His research interests have focused on the measurement and control of air pollution emissions from on-road and off-road vehicles and equipment powered by internal combustion engines. Mr. Springer has authored more than three dozen peer-reviewed technical papers and publications. He was elected a member of the National Academy of Engineering in 1996 and is a Fellow of ASME, a Fellow of SAE, and a Diplomate of the American Academy of Environmental Engineers. He was named Honorary Member of ASME in 2003 for developing test methods for measuring emissions of smoke, odor, and particulate matter from internal combustion engines and advancing this understanding through extensive publishing activity. He is a recipient of ASME's Honda Medal and Dedicated Service Award. He served on the National Academies Committee on Carbon Monoxide Episodes in Meteorological and Topographical Problem Areas and is a member of the Committee on State Practices in Setting Mobile Source Emissions Standards. He holds a BS in mechanical engineering from Texas A&M University and an MS in physics from Trinity University.

**Margaret A. Walls** is Resident Scholar at Resources for the Future (RFF). She was on the economics faculty of Victoria University, Wellington, New Zealand, from 1998 to 2000 and a Fellow in RFF's Energy and Natural Resources Division from 1987 to 1996. Her current research focuses on solid waste and recycling, urban land use, and air quality issues. She has published numerous articles that assess the efficiency and effectiveness of solid waste policies. In the area of transportation, Dr. Walls has modeled household vehicle ownership and use and the cost-effectiveness of various alternative fuels. She has published more than two dozen articles in refereed journals and a dozen book chapters on energy, waste disposal, and land use policies. She is a member of the American Economics Association and the Association of Environmental and Resource Economists. She holds a BS in economics from the University of Kentucky and a PhD in economics from the University of California, Santa Barbara.

**Joseph D. Walter** retired in 1999 as President and Managing Director of Bridgestone Technical Center Europe (Rome). He is now an Adjunct Professor in the College of Engineering at the University of Akron, where he teaches engineering mechanics courses. Before joining the Bridgestone Technical Center in 1994, he was Vice President and Director of Research at Bridgestone/Firestone, Inc. He began his career at the Firestone Tire and Rubber Company in 1966, where he held a series of technical and management positions of increasing responsibility. Dr. Walter has authored or coauthored more than two dozen journal articles and book chapters on aspects of tire mechanics, materials, design, and testing. He recently coedited the book *The Pneumatic Tire,* with a grant from the National Highway Traffic Safety Administration. He is a founding member of the Tire Society and is active in SAE, the American Chemical Society, and ASME. He was a member of the National Academies Committee on Fuel Economy of Automobiles and Light Trucks. He holds a BS, an MS, and a PhD in mechanical engineering from Virginia Polytechnic Institute and State University and an MBA from the University of Akron.

# Andrew Jackson

History Maker Bios

## Carol H. Behrman

⌐ LERNER PUBLICATIONS COMPANY • MINNEAPOLIS

*To my dear Rose  —C. H. B.*

*The publisher thanks Staff of The Hermitage, Home of President Andrew Jackson, for its assistance with this book.*

Lerner Publications Company
A division of Lerner Publishing Group
241 First Avenue North
Minneapolis, MN 55401 U.S.A.

Website address: www.lernerbooks.com

Library of Congress Cataloging-in-Publication Data

Behrman, Carol H.
    Andrew Jackson / by Carol H. Behrman.
        p. cm. — (History maker bios)
    Summary: Introduces the life of the "people's president," who spent his childhood on the frontier, his youth as a military hero, and his adulthood as a lawyer, judge, and politician.
    Includes bibliographical references (p.  ) and index.
    ISBN: 0–8225–1543–1 (lib. bdg. : alk. paper)
    1. Jackson, Andrew, 1767–1845—Juvenile literature. 2. Presidents—United States—Biography—Juvenile literature. [1. Jackson, Andrew, 1767–1845. 2. Presidents.] I. Title. II. Series.
    E382.B44 2005
    973.5'6'092—dc22                                        2003022743

Manufactured in the United States of America
1 2 3 4 5 6 – JR – 10 09 08 07 06 05

# TABLE OF CONTENTS

INTRODUCTION 5

1. A FRONTIER BOYHOOD 6

2. THE WILD YOUNG REBEL 16

3. LAW COMES TO TENNESSEE 21

4. GENERAL JACKSON 29

5. PRESIDENT OF THE PEOPLE 37

TIMELINE 44

THE HERMITAGE 45

FURTHER READING 46

WEBSITES 47

SELECT BIBLIOGRAPHY 47

INDEX 48

# Introduction

Andrew Jackson grew up on the American frontier as the son of poor farmers. He was a wild, fun-loving boy who often got into trouble. No one ever dreamed that he would be a great man someday. But Andy surprised them all. He became a brave general whose soldiers nicknamed him Old Hickory for his strength and courage. After he led the U.S. Army to victory at the Battle of New Orleans during the War of 1812 against Great Britain, he was called the Hero of New Orleans. Later, he served as the seventh president of the United States. But throughout his life, Andrew Jackson always remembered growing up poor. He fought for the plain, common folks, and they loved him.

This is his story.

# 1 A FRONTIER BOYHOOD

**A**ndy Jackson's mother and father, Elizabeth and Andrew, were immigrants from Ireland. When they came across the Atlantic Ocean in 1765, before Andy was born, there was no United States. Great Britain owned the American colonies.

The Jacksons and their two sons, two-year-old Hugh and five-month-old Robert, settled in the Waxhaws, a region in western North Carolina. Life was not easy on the frontier. The land was barren and scrubby—not good at all for farming. The Jacksons worked hard, but tragedy struck in February 1767. Andrew was badly hurt and died. One month later, on March 15, Elizabeth's third son was born. She named the boy Andrew after his father.

*Andy was born in a cabin probably like this one on March 15, 1767.*

Baby Andy and his brothers went with Elizabeth to live with their Aunt Jane and her family at their farm. Andy's mother helped take care of the family and the house. Everyone had lots of chores to do, but Andy worked hard and never complained. He didn't mind farmwork.

## THE WAXHAWS

When Andy Jackson grew up in the Waxhaws, not many people lived in this wild, rough place on North Carolina's western frontier. Bears and other wild animals roamed the woods. Boys learned to use guns at a young age. They hunted and fished to help feed their families. Many Native Americans also lived in the region. Their homes had been there before the white settlers had come, and sometimes they fought with settlers. All in all, life in the Waxhaws was dangerous. Its people had to be tough and independent.

Andy went to school in a one-room house like this one.

School was a different matter. The small schoolhouse that Andy went to had one room for students of all ages. There were no windows and no chairs. The children sat on logs. Andy would rather play with his friends than sit in the schoolroom. He often skipped class. He loved to wrestle and to ride horses. He was good at most games and usually won. But even when he was losing, Andy never gave up.

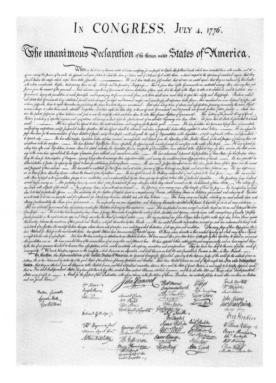

*Andy read a notice about the Declaration of Independence (LEFT). The declaration said that the American colonies were free of British rule.*

Andy also loved to play tricks on his pals, but sometimes he got angry when he was the butt of a joke. Once, when his friends made fun of him, he shouted, "By God, if one of you laughs, I'll kill him!"

Andy was popular despite his temper. And he was very good at one school subject: reading. Even many grown-ups could not read then. By the time Andy was nine, townspeople would gather around to hear him read the news. One summer day in 1776, he read an important notice about a Declaration of Independence.

Many people in the American colonies did not want to belong to Great Britain anymore. In the Declaration of Independence, a group of American leaders said that the colonies were free from British rule. People cheered at the words, "All men are created equal."

Americans were ready to fight for their freedom. The British would not give up their colonies without a war. Men from the Waxhaws and from all over the colonies joined the Continental Army, a force led by General George Washington.

General George Washington led the men of the Continental Army against the British during the American Revolution (1775–1783).

## Sparking the American Revolution

Great Britain's king ruled the American colonies, and he did not treat his American subjects well. He forced them to pay taxes that Americans called unfair, put them in prison if they objected, and sent soldiers to enforce his laws. Some colonists, called patriots, demanded justice, but the king ignored their requests. The colonists began to talk about separating from Great Britain. In 1776, leaders from all the colonies met in Philadelphia, Pennsylvania, and declared their independence. But before America could be free, a war had to be fought and won.

Andy and his friends wanted to fight the British too. But they were too young to go to war, so they pretended to be soldiers. The boys played with swords and rifles made from sticks. They longed to be old enough to really fight.

But real war was ugly. The British army won most of the battles at first, and many Americans died. In May 1780, Andy's oldest brother, Hugh, was killed. It was a terrible, sad day for the Jackson family.

Years of bloody war followed. Meanwhile, Andy grew tall and strong. When he was thirteen, he and his brother Robert joined the fight. Andy delivered important messages for officers in the Continental Army. He was proud to be a soldier at last.

Andy's brother Hugh died after this battle in South Carolina in 1780.

Then war came to the Waxhaws. When the British attacked their town, Andy and Robert had to escape into the woods. They hid all night long. But the next morning, British soldiers captured the boys.

When a British officer ordered Andy to polish his boots, Andy refused. He said that he was a prisoner of war, not a servant.

The officer's face turned red with anger. He raised his sword, and Andy threw up a hand to protect himself. The sword gashed his fingers and head as it came down. But Andy still wouldn't polish the officer's boots.

*Andy refused to shine a British officer's boots. His act of bravery and pride nearly cost him his life.*

Andy and Robert were thrown into a dirty, crowded prison, where they both became sick with smallpox. When their mother heard what had happened, she traveled many miles to plead with the British for the boys' freedom.

She convinced a British officer to release her sons. Robert died on the long, miserable journey home, and Andy was ill for a long time. "I was a skeleton," he said, but his mother tenderly nursed him back to health.

When Andy was well enough, his mother went to nurse other soldiers in Charleston, South Carolina. As she worked on ships crowded with ill and injured men, she caught the disease cholera. She died in 1781.

Andy never forgot his mother's words before she had left for Charleston. She had reminded him that he must always be honest and loyal. "Never tell a lie nor take what is not your own," he remembered her saying. Andy Jackson was fourteen years old. He was all alone in the world.

# 2 THE WILD YOUNG REBEL

**A**fter six years of war, the fighting in the American Revolution finally ended in 1781. The Americans had won. The British soldiers went home, and the colonies were free. Bells rang and people cheered in all the thirteen states.

Andy was proud of his part in the fight for freedom. But his mother and brothers were gone. He was lonely and confused. His relatives tried to help by taking Andy into their homes, but he never stayed long. He quarreled with everyone and hung out with a wild group of friends. They played cards and bet on horse races. Andy and his teenage pals were rowdy and careless. One of these friends described Andy, saying, "No boy ever lived who liked fun better than he."

*American colonists cheer the news of their victory over the British.*

It seemed to many people as though Andy Jackson had no ambition. He owed money everywhere and was in deep trouble. But his mother's teachings had not been in vain. Andy soon realized he was wasting his life. He decided to go back to school and make something of himself.

Andy worked as a teacher for a short time, but soon he was ready for something new. He decided to become a lawyer. Andy could learn the law if he could find a licensed attorney with whom to work and study.

## A DICEY PASTIME

One of Andy's risky habits was playing a dice game called Rattle and Snap. Andy often bet—and lost—money on the game. Once, when he was close to going to jail for his debts, he took one last chance. He bet his horse—his only valuable possession—and won. Andy paid off his debts and never played another round of dice.

*Andy learned the law by studying it in a law office like this one in Salisbury, North Carolina.*

Andy went to the large town of Salisbury, North Carolina. An important local attorney named Spruce McCay agreed to let Andy work for him and learn the law.

Andy studied with McCay for two years. He worked hard, but he also had time to find new friends. Once again, he became the leader of a fun-loving crowd. He was popular with both young men and young women. Andy was tall and handsome, with striking blue eyes and thick red hair.

In September 1787, Andrew Jackson finished his studies. Two judges tested him on his knowledge of the law. Andrew passed the test easily. At the age of twenty, he was officially qualified to work as a lawyer.

But there were already many lawyers in Salisbury. Andrew decided his chances of finding work were better somewhere else. He heard about a job opening for a lawyer in the Western District, an area that stretched westward to the Mississippi River. It was a rough, tough place, and many people were afraid to travel there. Andrew took the job. He was tough too. After all, he had grown up on the frontier.

Andrew set out on horseback with a few friends. He took along a rifle, two pistols, and his hunting dogs. Law books were stuffed into his pack. Andrew was on his way to take on the lawbreakers of the Western District.

# 3 LAW COMES TO TENNESSEE

Jackson's group headed for Nashville, a city in a part of the Western District that was later called Tennessee. The trip was long and dangerous. The travelers crossed over mountains and through wild, unfamiliar land.

*Jackson stands armed and ready to uphold the law on the frontier*

When they reached Nashville in 1788, it wasn't much of a town. It had only a few shabby stores, and the courthouse was falling apart. Even worse, some people didn't respect the law. But Jackson made sure that people obeyed the law—and that those who didn't paid for it. Once a criminal stamped hard on Jackson's foot. Jackson didn't hesitate. He swung a block of wood at the man and knocked him out.

The people of Nashville welcomed the tough new prosecutor. Soon the young lawyer had lots of business. He also had a comfortable new home. He rented rooms from the Donelsons, an important Nashville family. Jackson liked the Donelsons, especially their beautiful daughter, Rachel. She was living at home after leaving her husband. She and Andrew became friends and soon fell in love. They were married in August 1791. In 1794, they remarried after learning that their first marriage wasn't official.

*Andrew met his wife, Rachel Donelson, during his stay in Nashville.*

The busy U.S. capital city, Philadelphia, as it looked in about 1796

Twenty-four-year-old Jackson had a successful career and a loving wife. Eventually, he and Rachel developed a fine home and farm called the Hermitage. Meanwhile, the area around Nashville was growing, and in 1796, Tennessee became a state. The new state needed strong leaders. Jackson was elected to the House of Representatives in the U.S. Congress. He traveled to Philadelphia—the country's capital at that time—for meetings and government business.

It was important work. But Andrew was unhappy, and he missed Rachel.

Jackson left his job as a representative in 1797. But a few months later, he was back in Philadelphia as a senator. Jackson was glad to serve his country, but he still missed Rachel, and he needed to return to his law practice. In 1798, he quit and hurried home.

In 1804, Jackson made his home at the Hermitage.

*Judge Jackson (POINTING) orders a disrespectful criminal to give himself up. A crowd of Nashville residents looks on.*

Back in Nashville, Jackson was elected a judge. He took his new job very seriously. He told his juries to always "do what is right," and he kept up his tough reputation. A criminal once seized a gun and cursed at the judge and jury before charging out of the courthouse. Judge Jackson acted quickly. He stormed into the street after the man and flashed pistols in his face. "Surrender," he ordered, "or I'll blow you through." The man dropped his gun.

Jackson's quick temper flared up whenever he felt wronged. To defend his honor, he sometimes challenged men to gunfights. Jackson fought one duel after he became major general of the Tennessee militia, or state army. Another man who had wanted the job was angry. He insulted Andrew and Rachel. At the duel, both men drew their pistols. Fortunately, friends settled the fight before a single shot was fired.

But in 1806, a duel ended badly. Jackson won, but he killed the other man and was badly wounded himself. The duel left him with a bullet in his chest for the rest of his life, causing him great pain.

*Jackson, wounded during a duel in 1806, shot and killed his rival.*

*Jackson and Rachel adopted their nephew Andrew in 1809. They named him Andrew Jackson Jr.*

Andrew was happy and respected during these years. Just one thing was missing. He and Rachel had no children. In 1809, Andrew and Rachel adopted one of her brother's babies and named him Andrew Jackson Jr. They were thrilled to have a child.

Meanwhile, the United States was having trouble with an old enemy. In 1812, the young country found itself at war with Great Britain again.

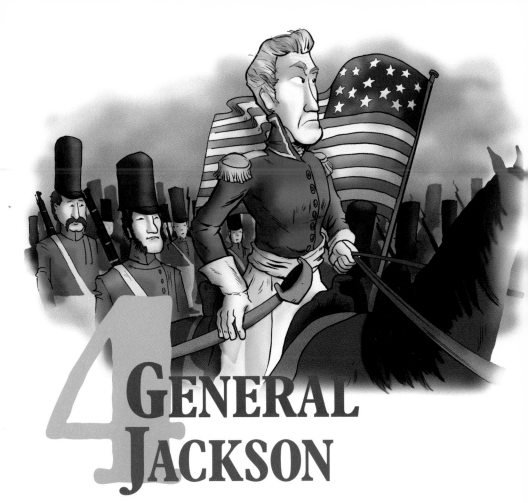

# 4 GENERAL JACKSON

**E**ven after the Revolution, Great Britain tried to treat the United States like a colony. U.S. ships weren't safe at sea. Captured U.S. sailors were forced to join the British navy. In the War of 1812, the new country fought for its rights again.

At first, the British were winning the war. They burned down the President's House in Washington, D.C., and captured other cities. Things looked bad for the United States.

Andrew Jackson had fought for his country as a teenager, and he wanted to help again. General Jackson called upon young men in Tennessee to join him. The men respected Jackson, and many were ready to follow him into battle.

The British attacked the new capital city of Washington, D.C., during the War of 1812.

*This 1815 painting is one of the first known pictures of Jackson. It shows how Major General Jackson looked when he led his men to New Orleans during the War of 1812.*

Jackson's troops waited months for orders. Finally, they were told to head to New Orleans. As people cheered and waved from shore on an icy December day, Jackson and his soldiers boarded riverboats and sailed to Natchez, Mississippi. They set up camp and waited for supplies, but none came. They ran out of food and medicine. The men were hungry and sick.

New orders finally came—telling Jackson to go home and to leave his troops to manage for themselves. General Jackson was angry. He would never abandon his men.

*Jackson offered his horse to his men during their journey back to Tennessee.*

Jackson led his ragged army on a tough five-hundred-mile trek. He gave his horse to sick men and told stories to keep their spirits up. Jackson's soldiers were grateful to their courageous general. They called him Old Hickory, because hickory wood was strong. After bringing his men safely home, Jackson was a local hero. One newspaper wrote, "Long will [their] General live in the memory of . . . West Tennessee."

In October 1813, Jackson finally got the chance to lead troops in battle. He was ordered to fight the Creek people, who were helping the British. Bloody battles followed, where hundreds of Creeks and many U.S. soldiers were killed. In 1814, U.S. forces won the Creek War, and General Jackson made the Creeks give up much of their land. The Creeks feared Jackson and called him Sharp Knife. However, Jackson could show pity as well as fierceness. He and Rachel adopted Lyncoya, a young Creek boy whose family had been killed in the war.

*Jackson talks about a peace agreement with Creek leader Red Eagle. The Creek people called Jackson Sharp Knife.*

Meanwhile, the British were nearing New Orleans. This important city's defenses were weak, and most people didn't think it stood a chance against Britain's powerful forces. But Jackson was determined to save the city. He traveled to New Orleans and began making plans for battle.

The British invaded in December 1814 with more soldiers and more guns than the U.S. forces had. But Jackson was not afraid, roaring, "I will smash them!" On January 8, 1815, the British attacked. Jackson's men were good shots, and they fired on the British troops from behind dirt walls.

*Jackson (STANDING CENTER) leads his men against the British during the Battle of New Orleans in 1815.*

*General Jackson was called the Hero of New Orleans for his fearless leadership during the Battle of New Orleans.*

The British were surprised by the Americans' skill in battle. Hundreds of British soldiers died, and the troops finally retreated. The United States had won the battle.

New Orleans held a grand parade to honor General Jackson. People across the country called him the Hero of New Orleans.

After the war, forty-eight-year-old Jackson was glad to go home to the Hermitage and his beloved Rachel. He settled down to care for his family and his farm.

But the general's skills were needed again. In 1817, the U.S. government asked him to capture land from the Seminole people in Florida. Spain owned Florida at the time, but Jackson's troops defeated the Seminoles and took control of the area. Spain sold Florida to the United States, and Americans called Jackson a hero.

In 1821, Jackson became Florida's governor. He and Rachel moved there, and Jackson worked to make laws that protected the people. But the Jacksons didn't like Florida, and they went home as soon as the new government was running well. They ran their farm and welcomed many visitors. Jackson hoped to spend the rest of his life there. But his country would need him one more time.

# 5 PRESIDENT OF THE PEOPLE

**T**he Jackson family had a big house and a prosperous farm. Life was easy at the Hermitage. But Jackson never forgot what it was like to grow up poor, and he worried that the government helped the rich and powerful too much. Someone had to protect the rest of the people. In 1828, at the age of sixty-one, Jackson ran for president.

Many powerful people didn't like Jackson and didn't want him to be president. Newspapers printed unkind things about him and Rachel. But the common people wanted him as their leader and elected him the seventh president of the United States.

It was time for the Jacksons to move to the President's House. But Rachel had been very ill, and the nasty remarks about her and Jackson had upset her terribly. Her health grew worse and worse. Just after the election, she had a heart attack. She died with her husband at her bedside. Jackson could not believe his beloved wife was gone.

Rachel was buried in the garden of the Hermitage. Jackson's heart was broken. But he had a job to do for his country.

On March 4, 1829, Jackson was sworn in as president. As the "people's president," he invited the public to the celebration. Thousands of people came, crowding the elegant President's House and getting it dirty with their muddy boots. But these were the people who had elected President Jackson, and he vowed to do all he could to help them and to make the nation strong.

Thousands of people came to cheer their new president.

Not all of Jackson's decisions were good for everyone. For example, like many Americans at the time, he didn't believe that Native Americans deserved the same rights as white people. In 1830, to please white settlers who wanted Native American land, Jackson signed the Indian Removal Act. The act forced Native American families to move westward across the Mississippi River. The trip was long and hard, and thousands of Native Americans died. This tragic journey became known as the Trail of Tears.

*Native Americans move westward under order of Jackson's Indian Removal Act. The journey is called the Trail of Tears.*

## States' Rights

President Jackson struggled with an issue called states' rights. Some southerners said that they shouldn't have to follow federal laws if they didn't agree with them. They claimed that the rights of the states were more important than the demands of the national government. But Jackson knew that the country would weaken if each state could obey some laws but not others. Jackson told southerners, "Our Union . . . must be preserved."

But President Jackson did all he could to help the common people and make the nation strong. He was reelected in 1832. During his eight years in office, he cut spending and paid off the national debt. He also tried to make the country bigger by adding the territory of Texas, then owned by Mexico. He failed. But American settlement in Texas continued.

This political cartoon shows Jackson closing the Bank of the United States. He called the bank a monster and crushed it.

Jackson faced one of his toughest challenges in his second term. He thought that the Bank of the United States was too big and powerful. Instead of this central bank, he wanted local banks for ordinary people around the country. He fought to close down the bank, and he finally won.

Jackson believed that, as the country's leader, he had a "sacred trust" to carry out the will of the people. He worked hard at that job, and Americans were grateful. When Jackson's presidency ended in 1837, he was the most popular president since George Washington. At seventy years of age, it was time for the old soldier to go home.

During Jackson's last years at the Hermitage, his old wounds often hurt him, and he had difficulty breathing. As always, he bravely ignored the pain. He still read newspapers and kept up with the country's affairs. He gave advice to new leaders, and visitors came from far and wide to see the great man. People respectfully called him "General."

The general's health finally gave out. Family and friends surrounded his bed. He told them not to cry, whispering, "We shall all meet in Heaven." Andrew Jackson died on June 8, 1845. The people's president was buried beside Rachel at the Hermitage.

*This photograph of Jackson was taken in 1844 or 1845, near the end of his life. His successful time as president is often called the Age of Jackson.*

# TIMELINE

## In the year . . .

| | | |
|---|---|---|
| 1780 | Andrew and his brother Robert were captured by British troops. | Age 13 |
| 1781 | Robert died of smallpox. Andrew's mother died of cholera. | |
| 1783–84 | he taught school in the Waxhaws. he studied law in North Carolina. | Age 17 |
| 1788 | he arrived in Nashville to work as a prosecutor in the Western District. | Age 21 |
| 1791 | he and Rachel were married. They remarried in 1794. | |
| 1796 | he was elected representative from Tennessee. | Age 29 |
| 1797 | he was elected senator from Tennessee. | |
| 1798 | he was elected a judge in Tennessee. | |
| 1802 | he became a major general of the Tennessee militia. | Age 35 |
| 1809 | he and Rachel adopted Andrew Jackson Jr. | |
| 1812 | the War of 1812 began. | |
| 1814 | his troops won the Creek War. | |
| 1815 | his troops defeated the British at the Battle of New Orleans. | Age 48 |
| 1821 | he became Florida's governor. | |
| 1828 | he was elected U.S. president. Rachel died at the Hermitage. | Age 61 |
| 1830 | he signed the Indian Removal Act. | |
| 1832 | he was reelected president. | Age 65 |
| 1845 | he died on June 8 and was buried next to Rachel. | Age 78 |

# THE HERMITAGE

Andrew Jackson and Rachel created a beautiful home near Nashville, Tennessee. They named it the Hermitage. It was part of a plantation—a large, southern-style farm—where they grew cotton. Slaves worked on the plantation and in the house. Many Americans believed that slavery was wrong. But Jackson and many other plantation owners disagreed. They depended on slaves to work their fields.

Andrew Jackson lived at the Hermitage for forty years. It was the place he loved best, and he shared many happy times at home with Rachel. "How often," he once said, "do my thoughts lead me back to the Hermitage." Both he and Rachel are buried there in the garden.

Modern tourists can still visit the Hermitage. It is kept just as it was when Jackson lived in it, with the same furniture and pictures on the walls. Jackson's eyeglasses, sword, and Bible are there. So is the special chair he used in his last years when he was ill. Visitors to the Hermitage get an idea of what life was like in the Age of Jackson.

# FURTHER READING

Landau, Elaine. *The President's Work: A Look at the Executive Branch.* Minneapolis: Lerner Publications Company, 2004. This book examines how presidents do their job.

Miller, Brandon Marie. *Growing Up in Revolution and the New Nation: 1775 to 1800.* Minneapolis: Lerner Publications Company, 2003. This book for older readers takes a look at life for kids like Andrew Jackson during and after the American Revolution.

Potts, Steve. *Andrew Jackson: A Photo-Illustrated Biography.* Mankato, MN: Bridgestone Books, 1996. This book tells Andrew's story with the help of photos and illustrations.

Sirvaitis, Karen. *Tennessee.* Minneapolis: Lerner Publications Company, 2003. Take a look at the state where Andrew Jackson spent most of his life.

Stefoff, Rebecca. *The War of 1812.* New York: Benchmark Books, 2001. This book explores the War of 1812, including the Battle of New Orleans.

Stein, R. Conrad. *The Trail of Tears.* Chicago: Children's Press, 1993. This book tells of the terrible journey made by Cherokee and other Native Americans after Andrew Jackson signed the Indian Removal Act.

Waxman, Laura Hamilton. *Sequoyah.* Minneapolis: Lerner Publications Company, 2004. Sequoyah was a Cherokee who lived during the time of the Trail of Tears. This biography takes a look at his life.

# WEBSITES

**Biography of Andrew Jackson**
<http://www.whitehouse.gov/history/presidents/aj7.html>
A biography of the seventh president is available at the official White House website.

**The Hermitage: Home of President Andrew Jackson**
<http://www.thehermitage.com>
This website offers a glimpse into the Hermitage, as well as information on how to visit there.

# SELECT BIBLIOGRAPHY

Andrist, Ralph K. *Andrew Jackson, Soldier and Statesman.* New York: American Heritage Publishing Co., 1963.

Davis, Burke. *Old Hickory: A Life of Andrew Jackson.* New York: Dial Press, 1977.

James, Marquis. *The Life of Andrew Jackson, Complete in One Volume.* New York: Bobbs-Merrill Company, 1938.

Remini, Robert V. *Andrew Jackson.* New York: Twayne Publishers, 1966.

Remini, Robert V. *The Life of Andrew Jackson.* New York: Harper and Row, 1988.

Schlesinger, Arthur M., Jr. *The Age of Jackson.* Boston: Little Brown, 1946.

Van Deusen, Glyndon G. *The Jacksonian Era, 1828–1848.* New York: Harper and Row, 1959.

# INDEX

American Revolution, 11–17

Bank of the United States, 42

Battle of New Orleans, 5, 34–35

birth, 7

childhood, 7–15

congressman, 24–25

Creek War, 33

death, 43

duels, 27

general, 27, 30–36

governor of Florida, 36

Great Britain, 5, 6, 11–16, 28–30, 33–35

Hermitage, 25, 35, 36, 37, 43, 45

Jackson, Andrew (father), 6–7

Jackson, Andrew Jr. (son), 28

Jackson, Elizabeth (mother), 6, 8, 15

Jackson, Hugh (brother), 7, 13

Jackson, Rachel (wife), 23–25, 28, 33, 35, 36, 38–39, 45

Jackson, Robert (brother), 7, 13–15

judge, 26

lawyer, 20–23

Lyncoya (son), 33

Nashville, 21–26

Native Americans, 8, 33, 36, 40

presidency, 5, 37–42

school, 9, 10

Seminoles, 36

states' rights, 41

temper, 10, 22, 26–27

Trail of Tears, 40

War of 1812, 5, 29–35

Washington, George, 11, 42

Waxhaws, 6–8, 11, 14

Western District, 20–24

## Acknowledgments

**The images in this book are used with the permission of:** Independence National Historical Park, p. 4; Tim Parlin, pp. 6, 14, 16, 21, 29, 37, 44; Tennessee State Museum Photographic Archives, p. 7; © North Wind Picture Archive, pp. 9, 13, 27, 30; courtesy of the National Archives, p. 10; courtesy of the Library of Congress, pp. 11 (LC-USZ62-45172), 17 (LC-USZC2-2131), 22 (LC-USZ62-02630), 26 (LC-USZ62-60870), 32 (LC-USZ62-5244), 34 (LC-USZC4-6222), 39 (LC-USZ62-1805), 42 (LC-USZ62-809), 43 (LC-USZC4-1807), 45 (LC-USZC4-1320); The Hermitage: Home of President Andrew Jackson, Nashville, Tennessee, pp. 14, 23, 25, 28, 33, 38; courtesy of Dover Publications, p. 19; © Brown Brothers, p. 24; Historic Hudson Valley, Tarrytown, New York, p. 31; © Eastern National/courtesy of the Horseshoe Bend National Military Park, p. 35; The Trail of Tears, by Robert Lindneux, Woolaroc Museum, Bartlesville, Oklahoma, p. 40. **Front cover:** courtesy of the Library of Congress (LC-USZC4-2109); illustrations by Tim Parlin. **Back cover:** courtesy of the Library of Congress (LC-USZ61-1453). **For quoted material:** p. 10, 15 (bottom), 26 (top), 41, 43, Marquis James, *The Life of Andrew Jackson, Complete in One Volume* (New York: Bobbs-Merrill Company, 1938); p. 11, *World Book Encyclopedia*, vol. 5, S.V. "Declaration of Independence"; p. 15 (top), Burke Davis, *Old Hickory: A Life of Andrew Jackson* (New York: Dial Press, 1977); p. 17, 26 (bottom), 32, 34, Robert V. Remini, *The Life of Andrew Jackson* (New York: Harper and Row, 1988); p. 42, Robert V. Remini, *Andrew Jackson* (New York: Twayne Publishers, 1966); p. 45, *The Ladies' Hermitage Association, The Hermitage, Home of President Andrew Jackson* (Hermitage, TN: The Ladies' Hermitage Association, 1997).